ORGANISING & DISORGANISING

A dynamic and non-linear theory of institutional emergence and its implications

Michael Thompson

Published in this first edition in 2008 by:
Triarchy Press
Station Offices
Axminster
Devon. EX13 5PF
United Kingdom

+44 (0)1297 631456
info@triarchypress.com
www.triarchypress.com

Many of the ideas presented in the book were originally published by the Norwegian Research Centre in Organization and Management under the title Inherent Relationality (Report 9608), © LOS-Senteret and Michael Thompson.

A catalogue record for this book is available from the British Library.

Cover design and image by Heather Fallows -
www.whitespacegallery.org.uk

ISBN: 978-0-9557681-4-9

Contents

For Anne
s.q.n.

PREFACE

A Week in Norway
and
an Afternoon at the London School of Economics

In the Summer of 1992 I found myself invited to Bergen, for a week, to talk about cultural theory.[1] Here, at last, was an opportunity to connect a line of thinking that has developed largely within anthropology to that vast community of political scientists, organisation theorists, management scientists and so on that concerns itself, one way or another, with institutions. It was, as they say, an education. I gave five seminars at the LOS Centre (The Norwegian Centre for Management and Organisation), each of which is discernible in this book, in which I tried to explain cultural theory in a way that, I hoped, would make sense to anyone who was interested in what is loosely called "the new institutionalism". Interest there certainly was, and there were plenty of questions: always a good sign. But I could not understand them! In many parts of the world that would have been the end of it - the bridge-building effort would have been judged a failure - but not in Norway.

Over endless cups of strong black coffee (and later, as is the Viking way, over similarly endless glasses of extraordinarily expensive beer) the obstacles to trans-disciplinary communication were gradually identified. I learnt about the great divide between the methodological individualists and the methodological collectivists, and I began to understand why it

---

1　Properly speaking, and as will soon become evident, it is a *theory of socio-cultural viability*, but as that is such a mouthful it has been shortened to cultural theory: a name that, it turns out, is a source of considerable confusion. For instance, Terry Eagleton - the eminent Marxist literary critic - is Professor of Cultural Theory at Manchester University but has probably never heard of this cultural theory! The name, however, is now stuck and there is little anyone can do about it (apart from explaining where it has come from and what the full name should be). The theory has also sailed under a few other flags: the *theory of plural rationality* (which is probably the best of the bunch), *grid/group theory* (the worst of the bunch, as is explained in chapter 9) and even *neo-Durkheimian institutional theory* (which, while perfectly correct, and helpfully acknowledging its intellectual origins, is hardly likely to catch on).

was that people who were interested in making the modern state work a little better were not over-enthused by my suggestion that they should treat any non-randomness (of behaviour or of belief) as an institution. And it slowly dawned on me that *the transaction* - and, in particular, the transaction theory of Fredrik Barth (a renowned Norwegian anthropologist) that had so influenced me as a student - was at the very heart of the thinking of those with whom I was trying to establish some connection.

What follows (but, for reasons I will now explain, not immediately) is the bridge that finally took shape: a structure that is largely held together by the transaction, its abutments, containing not a grain of methodological individualism *or* methodological collectivism, and its cables spun uncompromisingly from non-randomnesses. A funny-looking contraption, perhaps, but it does span the gap. The trouble with this bridge, I soon realised, was that it was *so* funny-looking that nobody wanted to venture onto it! And, since I could not think of any way of altering its appearance, it ended up just sitting there: an intriguing oddity devoid of intellectual traffic.

And so it might have remained had I not, some 15 years later, found myself invited to the London School of Economics and Political Science (the LSE) to give a talk to members of the European chapter of the Society for Organisational Learning (SOL-Europe). Hosted by the LSE's Complexity Group[2], the title I had been given was "Cultural Theory as a Theory of Learning", which indeed it is, though I had not really thought of it like that until I received this serendipitous prod. The audience, I knew, would be comprised of thoughtful and practical (and, in many instances, awesomely high-achieving) folk from business and industry: people who know a lot about what really goes on inside organisations.

How, then, could I explain the import of what I had been setting out, all those years before in Norway, for the down-to-earth challenge of finding better ways of arriving at decisions in a world that, I readily confess, I have only glimpsed from the outside? Daniels and lions' dens, grandmothers

---

2   This is a self-funding venture, led by Eve Mitleton-Kelly. As its name implies, it is concerned with the social and organisational implications of the newly-emerged science of complex systems: systems that are "far-from-equilibrium" and exhibit "order without predictability".

and sucked eggs, angels and rushing-in fools all came to mind, and I decided I had better stick to things I knew something about: *clumsiness* (about which I had just written a book) and *Himalayan uncertainty* (about which I had just written another book)[3]. To my surprise, and delight, this curious and seemingly unbusinesslike mix - a mix, moreover, in which cultural theory, though present, was scarcely visible - went down very well. Indeed, it transpired that what I had laid out with such trepidation was exactly what they had been looking for, and there was a gratifyingly strong demand for the video footage of my talk.

The only trouble was that the talk itself, being what John Maynard Keynes (1931) called an "essay in persuasion", said very little about the theory that underlaid it, yet had, I felt pretty sure, infused it with its persuasiveness. So the talk needed to be complemented by an exposition of theory, and in a way that would be intelligible to those who had found the talk itself so persuasive. The week in Norway and the afternoon at the LSE, I realised, had been in the wrong order: an error that has now been corrected in this book. Putting these two together, and in this reversed order, has also helped to make the cultural theory bridge itself less funny-looking: a transformation that has also been eased, over the intervening 15 years, by the gradual seeping of complex systems thinking into the mainstream of social science. Even so, it is still not entirely commonplace.

*   *   *

Is the individual prior to the social collectivity or is the social collectivity prior to the individual? Social scientists have argued over this since the birth of their field of enquiry, spinning two vast and mutually contradictory theoretical framings: *methodological individualism* and *methodological collectivism*. Students, if they are lucky, are offered the choice; if they are unlucky they find that the choice has already been made for them, one way in some universities and departments, the other way in other

---

3 References, and some explanation of these books' contents, are to be found in chapter 1.

universities and departments.[4] But, of course (and this is where cultural theory comes in), it is not just an either/or decision. There is a third, and splendidly even-handed, possibility: neither!

The individual, cultural theorists point out, is *inherently relational*; individuality is, to a considerable extent, something that we get from our involvement with others. In other words, almost all of social science has got itself hung up on a false dualism. How, then, do things look once we adopt this anti-dualist approach and, in so doing, consign the whole centuries-long debate over methodological individualism and methodological collectivism to the limbo of badly phrased questions? "Refreshingly different" is the short answer, and this, essentially, is the answer that is provided in chapter 1: the talk at the LSE. The longer answer - by way of organisation theory, the new institutionalism, conventional definitions of management, the theory of surprise, and the emerging field known as artificial life - is provided in the remaining chapters: the no longer quite so funny-looking bridge.

There is no such thing as an organisation, is the main message. There are only ways of organising and ways of disorganising: five ways of organising (the hierarchical, the individualistic, the egalitarian, the fatalistic and the autonomous), each of which is a way of disorganising the other four. Since each of these ways of organising needs the others, otherwise it would have nothing to organise itself against, subversion is inevitable. And if subversion is inevitable then good management must be concerned with *clumsiness*: with encouraging those subversions that are constructive for the pluralised totality and with discouraging those that are not. And if everything that is organised is plural - the by-product, as it were, of these five ways of organising - then the conventional definition of management as "management within an organisation" breaks down completely. All decision making, on this anti-dualist view, takes place between the ways of organising, never within just one of them. But I am jumping ahead too fast. This is the funny-looking bridge and I need, first, to set out the essay in persuasion that, if I am lucky, will render that bridge less funny-looking.

---

4   Economics, especially in the United States, is firmly in the methodological
     individualist camp, as is psychology (except when there is talk of "distributed
     cognition"). Anthropology and sociology are more likely to be in the methodological
     collectivist camp. But it is often a wiggly and ever-changing line.

CHAPTER 1

Clumsiness: Why Isn't it as Easy
as Falling off a Log?

Arsenal Football Club's stadium is (or, rather, was) located in Highbury: the district, within the London Borough of Islington, where I live. So I was rather well-placed to observe the intriguing goings-on that led, just a few years ago, to it no longer being there. Arsenal and the Borough of Islington are, to put it mildly, very closely bound up with one another, and the Highbury Stadium is (or, rather, was) about as hallowed a piece of ground as one could hope to find, after perhaps the Wailing Wall in Jerusalem, or the Hajj Square in Mecca, or Bodhnath Stupa in Kathmandu. The trouble was that the pitch was slightly undersized (it could not be used for international matches)[5] and the stadium, now that standing is no longer permitted for safety reasons, could hold only 30,000 spectators. Arsenal, if it was to make the most of its status as one of the premier football clubs in the world, would have to have a full-sized pitch and room for at least 60,000 spectators.

Thus it was that, just a few years ago, Arsenal (I'll call it the *market actor)* sidled up to Islington Council (the *hierarchical actor*) with the suggestion that the council give the go-ahead - "outline planning permission", that is - for Arsenal to acquire, and demolish, the two streets of terraced houses immediately adjacent to its stadium, thereby enabling it to expand to a capacity of 60,000, along with a full-sized pitch. Within less than 24 hours of this approach becoming public knowledge, a third actor emerged - the Highbury Community Association. It, of course, was bitterly opposed to these plans. Some, but by no means all, of its members lived in the threatened houses, and many of them (as they were careful to point out) were also loyal Arsenal supporters. They were therefore in favour of Arsenal, and in favour of Arsenal staying in the

---

5   Matches between national teams, that is; matches between clubs from different
     countries can be played there. England, of course, would normally play at
     Wembley, but Arsenal would like to have a stadium that could host some World
     cup games if that tournament was being held in England.

Borough of Islington, but they were implacably opposed to the solution Arsenal was proposing: the *only* solution, Arsenal insisted, playing what it thought was its trump card, if the club was to remain in the borough.[6]

So this third actor - I'll call it the *egalitarian actor* (its arguments being largely couched in terms of the unfair treatment of residents, small businesses, the unemployed and so on) - really put the cat among the pigeons. An enormous controversy blew up, a petition with thousands of signatures was delivered to Islington Town Hall, and there was a vigorous television debate (chaired by the Conservative MP and one-time cabinet minister, Anne Widdecombe). It soon became very clear that there was no way Arsenal was going to get permission to expand on its Highbury site. A vast regeneration project, two miles away, around King's Cross and St Pancras Stations, was then identified as a possibility. It lay just inside the adjoining borough of Camden, but an inter-borough deal might be possible that would re-draw the boundary such that the new stadium would still be within Islington. But the developers said "no". They were committed to an up-market and high-rent redevelopment: one in which a vast stadium that would only be used every 10 days or so had no place. So it began to look as though Arsenal would indeed have to move right out of the borough: all the way out to near the M25 orbital road - way to the north, where the club has its training grounds (and where most of the players have bought their somewhat lavish houses).

But then two commercial property surveyors, who also happened to be fanatical Arsenal supporters, got out their maps. To everyone's amazement (including theirs), they found a triangular piece of rather low-rent and under-used land, bounded on two sides by busy railway lines, that would comfortably take a 60,000 seat stadium. Even more amazingly, it was less than half a mile from the old stadium and its hallowed (but under-sized) turf!

---

6   These three actors are somewhat simplified here, in the sense that some members
     of the Highbury Community Association may be rather more market-oriented
     characters (Nimbies, as they are sometimes called - Not In My Back Yard) whose
     primary aim is to protect the value of their houses. Also Arsenal itself, thanks to
     its over-close relationship with Islington Council, is not so full-blooded a market
     actor as are the two commercial property surveyors who discovered the site that
     Arsenal has now moved to. In other words, for simplicity, I am for the moment
     avoiding dealing with the various "pairwise alliances" that are possible.

In August 2006 (just 4 years later; on-time and on-budget) Arsenal moved into its new stadium: onto this near-ideal site the very existence of which had remained completely unnoticed until the three-cornered battle - the club, the borough and the community - had been joined! (See Figure 1.1.)

☐ *Arsenal Football Club* has got its state-of-the-art 60,000-seater stadium (and a handsome price for its old stadium, which is being redeveloped for housing).

☐ *Islington Council* has kept the club in the borough (and extracted a colossal "planning gain" - thousands of new homes, offices, a futuristic waste-transfer and recycling centre, some badly-needed public open space, and so on).

☐ The *Highbury Community Association* has saved the streets and houses around the old stadium, and forced the council to ensure that those businesses displaced by the new stadium were re-located within the borough, and without any loss of jobs. Of course, they are still critical - especially over the failure to build a new tube station within the stadium (the Piccadilly Line passes directly beneath it) - but they do have the satisfaction of knowing that the new stadium is the greenest in the world![7]

---

7   There is no provision for private car parking; almost all fans arrive and leave by public transport or on foot. Hi-tech ventilation minimises the need for air conditioning, solar panels generate electricity and green roofs provide biodiversity and insulation. Rainwater is collected and stored for re-use in irrigation and toilet flushing, and the re-use and re-cycling of the materials in the demolished buildings in the construction of the new stadium has cut the amount of waste going into landfill by 70%. [As entertainingly reported by Julia Stephenson: "Now football's gone eco-friendly, I'm a fan". *The Independent* (London) 27 March 2006. p.43.]

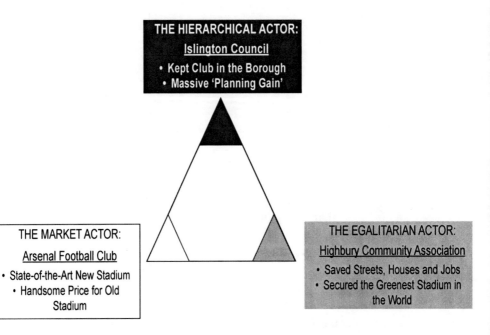

Figure 1.1: An Eminently Clumsy Solution

This outcome - in which each "apex" gets more of what it wants (and less of what it does not want) than if it had somehow managed to achieve hegemony and "go it alone" - is a nice example of what is now called a *clumsy solution*. And this chapter - this "essay in persuasion" - is about why this sort of solution is so rare, and why it is that we keep on and on saddling ourselves with the deeply unsatisfactory *elegant solutions*: outcomes, that is, that are arrived at by decision-making processes in which one or more of these three "voices" are excluded. Then, having answered those questions, I will conclude by saying something about how we might shift ourselves across from elegance to clumsiness.

So let me now give an example of what we usually get, especially when (as is very often the case) there is a major *scientific input* to the decision-making process. Back in the early 1980s, the United Nations Environment Programme (UNEP) asked the Austria-based International Institute for Applied Systems Analysis (IIASA) to provide it with a "systems overview" of the entire environment-and-development problem in the Himalayan Region, UNEP having just been mandated, by the United Nations General Assembly, with responsibility for this "environmental hotspot". The task was eventually delegated to me, together with a research assistant (Michael Warburton) and a summer student (Tom Hatley). Our report to UNEP, considerably expanded, was published (Thompson, Warburton and Hatley 1986) as a book: *Uncertainty On A Himalayan Scale*. This book has recently been republished (2007), with a new introduction, and with IIASA (and Oxford University's James Martin Institute) "ownership". The republication is by a Nepali publisher - Himal Books - and it is in their *Classics Series*.

But it was seen as anything *but* classic at the time. Indeed UNEP complained to IIASA that our report was "completely useless", and IIASA's deputy director (responsible for the institute's environment work) agreed, calling it "academic bullshit". Since I had resisted pressure from a concerned Program Leader to give UNEP something less "literary" and more like what they were expecting, and since another Program Leader had complained loudly that, thanks to me, it was impossible to get any more research funding from UNEP, IIASA's director, C.S. ("Buzz") Holling, was forced to bow to demands that I be dismissed. Fortunately, those who were baying for my blood accepted his suggestion that there should first be a report on me and my work by a respected member of IIASA's staff. He chose as the report-writer, Brian Arthur, who he knew (but the others did not) had also been the subject, just a year or two earlier, of demands that *he* be dismissed (because of his now classic work on increasing returns to scale [e.g. Arthur 1989]). So of course Brian wrote a glowing report - I still have it, in a file labelled "IIASA Oddities" - and I survived, but only just!

In other words, it is very difficult to get what is now called *uncomfortable knowledge* (Rayner 2006) up onto the table, as it were; and very, very easy to suppress it. Indeed, in an institutional setting such as IIASA it usually suppresses itself. And, without uncomfortable knowledge, you will not get clumsy solutions. That is why they are so rare.

*   *   *

So let us now have a look at what it was about this knowledge that was *so* uncomfortable, and at what was happening to policy in this Himalayan Region when only comfortable scientific knowledge was guiding and informing the decision-making process:

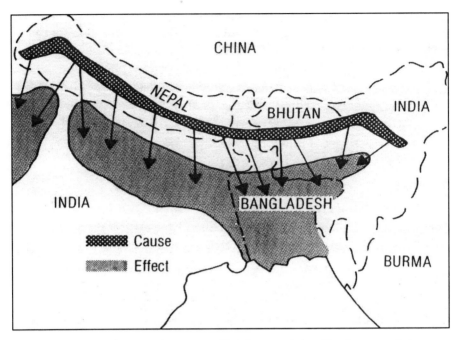

Figure 1.2: The Himalayan Region and the Environmental Orthodoxy

What our report did was challenge what is now called an "environmental orthodoxy" (e.g. Forsyth 2003, Leach and Mearns 1996); an orthodoxy, moreover, that has provided the basis for decades-worth of research and development aid in the whole region. At the centre of this orthodoxy there stands that anti-paragon, the Ignorant and Fecund Peasant - the Himalayan hill-farmer, whose predilection for large families, together with his inability to comprehend the environmental consequences of that predilection, is the root-cause of the rampaging and ever-worsening degradation that stretches all the way from the forests and pastures of the high Nepal Himalaya, through the teeming and fertile plains of India, to the vast delta of those great rivers - the Ganges and the Brahmaputra - that, over the millennia, have actually created most of Bangladesh (the delta) and, by spreading silt to a depth of some 5,000 metres, the plains too.

To understand this orthodoxy, and the wholly unwarranted "discourse of crisis" that it has engendered among those who have fallen under its thrall, we must travel back to 1972, to the United Nations Stockholm Environment Conference. It was at this conference that the problem was convincingly and authoritatively defined in terms of *population growth*. Erik Eckholm, who shortly afterwards wrote the influential book *Losing Ground* (1976), put it like this:

Population growth,,, is forcing farmers onto ever steeper slopes, slopes unfit for sustained farming even with the astonishingly elaborate terracing practised there. Meanwhile, villagers must roam further and further from their homes to gather fodder and firewood, thus surrounding most villages with a widening circle of denuded hillsides. Ground-holding trees are disappearing fast among the geologically young, jagged foothills of the Himalaya, which are among the most easily erodable anywhere. Landslides that destroy lives, homes and crops occur more and more frequently throughout the Nepalese hills.

Here then, in stark outline, was the problem: an increasing population is having to support itself on a resource base that it is actually causing to decline. Nor is this the end of Nepal's problems. As the resource base slides away from under its farmers, it causes havoc in the downstream countries of India and Bangladesh (as is indicated by the hatched strip in Figure 1.2).

Topsoil washing down into India and Bangladesh is now Nepal's most precious export but one for which it receives no compensation. As fertile soil slips away, the productive capacity of the hills declines, even while the demand for food grows inexorably. Even more ominously, farmers [because of the firewood crisis] have seen no choice but to adopt the self-defeating practice of burning dung for fuel.

Nor, according to this orthodoxy, is it just themselves that the Nepalis are defeating. As they propel ever more topsoil into their mountain torrents, Eckholm asserts, they render the reservoirs and hydropower stations in India useless with startling rapidity, they provoke worse flooding in both India and Bangladesh, and they raise the riverbeds to such an extent as to cause the river-courses to "meander about, often destroying prime farmland as they go". The Eckholm/Stockholm verdict was that Nepal was headed for total ecological and economic collapse within ten years at the most.

This "10 years to collapse" story was then told again and again, along with a multitude of research projects aimed at putting precise figures on the two key variables in the primary vicious circle: the *per capita fuelwood consumption rate* and the *sustainable yield from forest production.*

❑ We collated these studies (or, rather, expanded the collation that had already been carried out by a researcher at the US-based Institute of Current World Affairs), thereby revealing the true extent of the uncertainty:

Key variables	Factor by which expert estimates vary
Per capita fuelwood consumption	67
Sustainable yield from forest production	150 (x factor by which estimates of forest area vary)

Figure 1.3: The Only Table Of Quantitative Data In Our Report To UNEP

❑ From this we concluded that, if the most pessimistic estimates were correct, the Himalaya would become as bald as a coot overnight; and that, if the most optimistic estimates were correct, they would shortly sink beneath the greatest accumulation of biomass the world has ever seen! It was that conclusion - that piece of uncomfortable (but incontrovertible) knowledge - that was the source of all the trouble.

Since then, we have been able to gather and collate some of the many tellings of this "10 years to collapse" story. That little piece of knowledge-creation, it turns out, is even more uncomfortable. For instance, we found that David Attenborough had told exactly the Eckholm/Stockholm story in the course of making his acclaimed television series *The Natural World*:

We walked across hillsides in Nepal that have been stripped of their trees for firewood. Rain had gouged deep ravines down them, carrying away the soil, and the people were going hungry. A thousand miles away, in the delta of the Ganges, that same soil is being deposited, clogging the river channels. During the rainy season, the water, no longer held back by the forests, rushes down the rivers and floods the delta. Hundreds of people drown and thousands lose their fields and the homes.

And Britain's Overseas Development Agency (ODA) had said exactly the same, in the course of setting out its *Renewable Natural Resources Research Strategy*.[8]

The growing population's requirement for more food leads to clearing of forests to provide more land for crop production. Soil becomes exposed and is easily washed away by heavy monsoon rainfall. Land productivity quickly declines, leading to a demand for more land on which to produce crops...

With such unanimity, from such deeply-involved and knowledgeable actors, together with all the scientific expertise they are able to muster and all the research they are able to commission, you might well assume that this population growth-driven story is true, were it not for the timings of these gloom-laden pronouncements:

      Stockholm/Eckholm   1972

      David Attenborough   1984

      Overseas Development Agency 1997

The orthodox definition, we can now see, has the Overseas Development Agency standing on the very edge of an environmental abyss that is the self-same abyss that David Attenborough was standing on the edge of 13 years earlier and which, in its turn, is the self-same abyss that Erik Eckholm was standing on the edge of 12 years before that. How fortunate

---

8   The ODA (now re-named DfID - Department for International Development) is one of the largest providers of official development aid in the Himalayan region. It has an enormous office building in Kathmandu, with a fleet of gas-guzzling Land Rovers in DfID livery lined up on its forecourt.

for all of them that they should have been there, in Nepal, at just that climactic moment, and how strange that they should have been there 13 and 12 years apart, over a period of 25 years in all, when the collapse was due to happen within, at the most, 10 years!

So in our 2007 republication of this book, we were able to set out this even more uncomfortable piece of knowledge, and then go on to summarise the harm that has been done by all these policy actors (and their compliant scientists) who have persisted with the comfortable knowledge: the environmental orthodoxy.

- **The World Does Not Come To An End**

  With the environmental apocalypse it predicts having now been postponed at least three times, the orthodox definition really is way past its sell-by date. Indeed, if the institutions that still stock it - Britain's ODA (now DfID - Department for International Development), for instance - were supermarkets, they would have gone out of business, or been closed down by the health inspectors, long ago.

- **Blame The Victim: The Hill Farmer**

  In seeing the Himalayan farmer as an ignorant and fecund peasant, the orthodox definition blames the victim, thereby ruling out any consideration of how, and to what extent, he or she can be part of the solution. It is therefore seriously out of step, not just with those (like us) who are eager to write the obituaries for the Age of Aid,[9] but also with current thinking within the development community. *Social capital, civil society* and *good governance* - the New Millennium shibboleths of the World Bank and its ilk - would simply be non-starters if Nepal's citizens (more than three-quarters of whom are small-scale farmers) were ignorant and fecund peasants.

---

9   Which runs for roughly half a century: from the Bretton Woods Agreement in the immediate aftermath of the Second World War to the collapse of the Soviet Union. "Us", here, refers to myself and Dipak Gyawali (see Thompson and Gyawali, 2007).

□ **Gratuitous Heightening of Regional Tensions**

By pinning the silting-up of Indian dams and Bangladeshi
water channels, and the worsening floods and droughts that
have beset downstream communities all the way from Bihar
to the Sunderbans, on the axe-wielding zeal of the Nepali hill-
farmer, the orthodox definition has encouraged and justified
finger-pointing and sabre-rattling throughout a region that is,
at the best of times, far from being a haven of international
harmony, when in fact there are *none* of these man-made trans-
boundary risks.[10]

□ **Undermining of Nepal's Fragile Democracy**

And in Nepal itself, the orthodox definition has distorted the
development process - particularly through the justification it
provides for large-scale water-engineering projects as a panacea
to this mistaken view of environmental degradation - to the point
where the country's hard-won democracy is in danger of being
destroyed. Indeed, in some estimations, it has now become a
"failed state". The argument here is that development aid has
severely distorted the triangular interplay of the three forms of
solidarity: to the point where each ends up undermining its own
morality (*dharma* gone wrong, as Nepalis put it). Hierarchical
actors, forgetting all about the common good and the imperative
that they rise above narrow group and personal interests, devote
all their energies to what is euphemistically called "rent-
seeking"; market actors, forgetting all about Adam Smith's
"invisible hand", prosper even when others do not benefit (a
state of affairs dubbed "Licence Raj"); and egalitarian actors, no
longer Edmund Burke's "small platoons" springing up from the
grassroots, turn out to be front organisations for this unseemly
hierarchy/market stitch-up (BONGOs, DONGOs, GONGOs
and PONGOs as they are called; Business-Organised, Donor-

---

10   Bihar is the impoverished and notoriously ill-governed Indian state immediately
     downstream of Nepal. The Sunderbans are Bangladesh's tiger-infested islands of
     silt that mark the end of the Ganges Delta (above sea level, that is; the delta itself
     extends much further and the plume of silt is visible hundreds of kilometres out
     into the Bay of Bengal).

Organised, Government-Organised and Party-Organised Non-Governmental Organisations respectively). Democracy, it is reasoned, is simply not viable with this degree of distortion.

Putting all this together, we can say that this is science-for-policy at its most truly abysmal. Better - much, much better - to have done nothing at all than to have done what all those well-intentioned actors have done!

*   *   *

So the big question is: How can we, as the scientists who provide the science-for-policy, avoid getting ourselves into this sort of ghastly, and all too common, situation? "By ensuring that uncomfortable knowledge is not excluded", is the answer, of course. But how on Earth do you do that if everything is set up, institution-wise, so as to ensure that uncomfortable knowledge does not get a look-in?

Avoiding the Truly Abysmal: the First Steps Along the Elegance-to-Clumsiness Transition

The whole seemingly intractable problem of how to get uncomfortable knowledge into an institutional setting that is pretty well programmed to exclude it can be rephrased as follows: "Can we get the sort of clumsiness that led, more or less by accident, to Arsenal's new stadium to happen *by design*?". The answer, we will see, is "Yes, we can", but it requires research institutes such as IIASA to go about their business in a very different way. They need to back off from elegance - single definitions of problem and solution, clear separation of facts and values, reliance on optimisation, etc. - so as to be able to listen to "other voices". And to do that they are going to need *methods* that will tell them when some of these voices that they should be listening to are not being heard. A bit like Sherlock Holmes and "The Dog That Did Not Bark"!

And, to be fair, this is exactly what is beginning to happen at IIASA (and elsewhere: Oxford University's James Martin Institute for Science and Civilization, for instance). Indeed, as well as the re-published book *Uncertainty On A Himalayan Scale*, there is another recent book - *Clumsy Solutions For A Complex World* (Verweij and Thompson 2006) - that is very much an IIASA (and JMI) volume and that explains, with a host of examples, why it is that we need to move across from elegance to clumsiness, and how to actually do it.

So, with all that work already available, let me conclude by explaining a very recent bit of theory-cum-methodology that makes explicit the crucial link between clumsiness and democracy: a way of pinning down just what it is that distinguishes the sort of decision-making pursued by the likes of UNEP and Britain's ODA in the Himalaya from the sort of decision-making that gave us Arsenal's new stadium. And I should mention that this is the work of one of my IIASA-connected colleagues, Steven Ney (Ney 2006). What we need (and what Steven Ney has now given us) is some rigorously-argued yet practical way of characterising the absolute pits - science-for-policy at its very worst (as with the environmental orthodoxy in the Himalaya) - in relation to where we want to be: the sort of clumsy and multi-vocal engagement that gave us Arsenal's new stadium.

Put like that, we can see that the "absolute pits" corresponds to what Robert Dahl - the propounder of the classic theory of pluralist democracy - called *closed hegemony*: one voice drowning out all the others. And the exact opposite of that - the situation in which all the voices (a) have *access* and (b) are *responsive* to one another - is *pluralist democracy* or, in our terminology, *clumsiness*.[11] What Steven Ney has done is "refurbish" Dahl's classic (and essentially dualistic) scheme by specifying the three voices - the market voice, the hierarchical voice and the egalitarian voice - and then using them to place three "calibrations" on each of Dahl's axes:

---

11   Or rather, cultural theorists argue, this is what Dahl *should* have been saying.
Lacking a typology, however, he ended up equating voices with interests, as
in Arthur Bentley's (1949) dictum "There is no group without its interests".
Pluralism, in consequence, became just the latest historical version of the
individualistic (or market) model of democracy, with the other two models
- so vital to the constructive triangular interplay that cultural theorists see as
fundamental to democracy - disappearing from view.

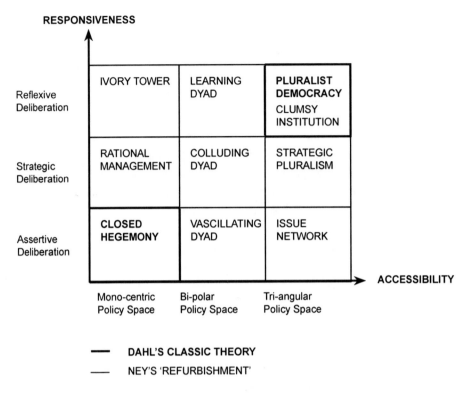

Figure 1.4: Classic Pluralist Theory Refurbished

Without going into the details of every square province, we can see that this 3 x 3 scheme enables us to go beyond Dahl's "either you've got it (pluralist democracy) or you haven't (closed hegemony)" and to distinguish varying degrees of better and worse. Moreover, we can now see that closed hegemony can come in three distinct forms (depending on which of the three voices is drowning out the other two) whilst *clumsy institution* - the most plural form of democracy - comes, as with Tolstoy's happy families, in just one form (all three voices are heard and responded to by the others). So this refurbished scheme copes with what would otherwise be a rather large "excluded middle". As Ney points out, few if any "policy sub-systems" (in the European Union anyway, not the Himalaya) are *so* undemocratic as to make it all the way down into the closed hegemony province, and, in the other direction, few if any are *so* democratic as to make it all the way up into the clumsy institution province.

This talk of "up" and "down" alerts us to the fact that there is, of course, a third dimension here - Ney calls it *deliberative quality* - and this means that our 3 x 3 matrix, far from being flat, is a curvy landscape in which the pits really *are* down there, and the tops up here:

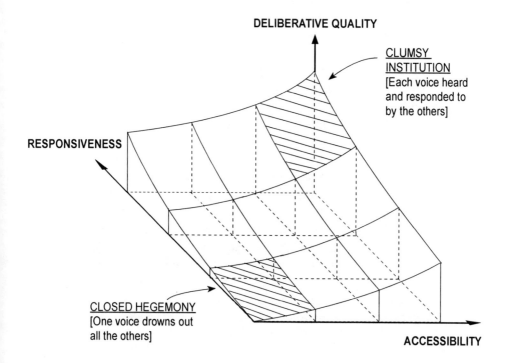

Figure 1.5: The Refurbishment With The Third Dimension Made Explicit

We can now see that my Himalayan tale of truly abysmal science-for-policy has been nicely chosen so as to map onto the lowest province within this landscape. And, in the other direction, the Arsenal story maps onto the loftiest province. Ney, in looking at policy sub-systems within Europe, has shown how it is possible (once you have acquired the requisite skills) to assign them to this or that particular province between these two extremes. And, once we have done that, we can do two things:

□   We can quite precisely specify what is needed to make policy systems more democratic. Any move that is *up*hill (and there are, in all, five altitudinal zones within this landscape) will be an improvement (if we value democracy and deliberative quality, that is). And, since there may often be some serious institutional obstacle to such a move, this scheme also enables us to identify various round-the-corner ways of achieving this improvement should it not be achievable directly.[12]

□   We can also identify faulty policy advice: advice that, if followed, would actually move the policy sub-system *down*hill. For instance, an influential normative argument in European pension policy is that we are suffering from too much pluralism: the "veto powers" wielded by all the actors who currently enjoy access have resulted in a sort of paralysis - a *Reformstau* - with the result that it is simply impossible to achieve any of the reforms that are so badly needed. With the benefit of this landscape, however, we can see that this advice, if heeded, would actually shift policy subsystems that are currently up in the third or fourth altitudinal zones down into the second or third: the very opposite of what is needed (as is confirmed when we look at those few European instances where rapid reform *has* taken place where, in every case, it has been triggered by an increase in either access or responsiveness, or both).

Another example, from industry, was the advice Unilever was getting from its trusted consultants on how best to deal with "Green" campaigns against some of its household products. The Greens, it was argued, were gunning for the chemical industry and had latched onto Unilever and its household products as presenting the most vulnerable chink in that industry's armour. Had Unilever followed that advice, and seen the Greens as "the enemy", it would have sought to silence the egalitarian voice, thereby moving itself down the landscape from the quite high position on the "deliberative quality dimension" that it at that time (early 1990s) was

---

12   If you re-draw Figure 1.5 as a number of square columns of increasing height you will see that a large number of ascending paths can be accessed by first nipping sideways, left or right, across the altitudinal zone you happen to be in. And this can be repeated if you run into another institutional obstacle once you have moved up into the next altitudinal zone. And of course, *in extremis,* you could even risk an initial move downwards: "reculer pour mieux sauter", as they say in Spain.

occupying. Fortunately, other counsels prevailed and Unilever elected to see the Greens as "dissatisfied customers", rather than the enemy. And, once they had done that, they became keenly interested in just why the Greens were dissatisfied and, more importantly, in how the corporation might re-design some of its products so as to lessen that dissatisfaction. All kinds of new product opportunities (the entire "Dove" range of toiletries, for instance) then revealed themselves (rather in the way that Arsenal found its hitherto hidden "ideal site") and Unilever moved itself even further up the landscape.[13]

Finally, equipped with this sort of methodology, you are much less likely to find yourself sacked! Uncomfortable knowledge becomes much less uncomfortable once you are able to show your "client" where he/she is currently on this landscape, how (for all sorts of readily understandable reasons) he/she came to be there, and what sorts of step-by-step transitions he/she could initiate so as to move further away from the gloomy depths of closed hegemony and towards the sunlit uplands of clumsy institution.

---

13   A more detailed analysis of this, in relation to Unilever's Frish lavatory rim
     blocks, is set out in Schwarz and Thompson (1990, chapter 1).

CHAPTER 2

Not Starting in the Obvious Place

Though there is no explicit mention of cultural theory in the preceding "essay in persuasion", it *is* there: in the triangular interplay of the market actor (Arsenal Football Club), the hierarchical actor (Islington Council) and the egalitarian actor (the Highbury Community Association). These three correspond to what are sometimes called the three "active" solidarities of cultural theory: *individualism*, *hierarchy* and *egalitarianism*, respectively. Nor, though the term "solidarity" may be somewhat abstract, is there anything disembodied about these actors. The Highbury Community Association is comprised of real flesh-and-blood people (myself amongst them; at any rate, I was present at its inaugural meeting) and the same is true of Arsenal Football Club and Islington Council.

Nor does a person's involvement in one form of solidarity disqualify him or her from involvement in others. Most (more likely, all) of those who came together in the Highbury Community Association, for instance, did not carry that pattern of social involvement across to their workplaces, or even to the functioning of their households. So the labels "individualist", "hierarchist" and "egalitarian" refer to those who, at times and in places, are acting so as to uphold these different forms of solidarity; they are not "personality types". In other words, there is nothing "individual" about them. Indeed, it makes more sense to see them as *dividuals*,[14] and that is what cultural theory strives to do.

I say "strives", because seeing things in this dividualistic way is not easy. Each of us, moreover, *is* a psycho-physiological entity and, in that important sense, an individual, and cultural theory is certainly not trying to deny that. But, if our focus is to be on the various patterns of relationships that we bind ourselves into, and if specific individuals turn up as nodes within more than one of those patterns, then we need to avoid seeing the individual as the "fundamental particle". And, if

---

14   The term "dividual" was coined by Marriott (1967) to convey the point that there is nothing socially indivisible about the individual.

we take that avoiding action, then we part company with all those - the methodological individualists *and* the methodological collectivists - who have set off from the obvious and everyday distinction - false dualism, we would say - between the individual and the society: the part and the whole.

Moreover, solidarities - the variously patterned ways in which we bind ourselves to one another - have a sort of *fractal* quality,[15] in that they are evident at every scale level: all the way from the global (the international regimes, for instance, that aim to manage things like the ozone layer, nuclear proliferation, climate change and world trade)[16] to the most local (styles of consumption within the household, for instance, or even the cognitive processes within the psycho-physiological entity).[17] So, if we were to do what most of social science does, and make a fundamental distinction between the individual and the society - the micro and the macro - then we would be slicing right through all these patterns that are what actually lace the whole caboodle together. Aggregating up (methodological individualism, as in efforts to arrive at a best social choice starting from disparate individual values)[18] and disaggregating down (methodological collectivism, as in the much relied-upon notion of *per capita consumption*)[19] make no sense at all if micro and macro, far from being separable, are each the cause of the other.

---

15   Fractals, most famously associated with Mandelbrot (1977), have a sort of infinite regress. Coastlines, for instance, as you zoom in on them, reveal equally convoluted micro-coastlines; on and on.

16   Most of the case study chapters in Verweij and Thompson (2006) are at this sort of scale.

17   An example at this sort of small scale would be Dake and Thompson (1999).

18   Famously shown by Arrow (1951/1963) to be impossible, given certain explicit assumptions.

19   Dividing one macronumber (national consumption) by another macronumber (national population) would be valid if the population was what statisticians call "homogenous". Cultural theory, of course, insists that it is "heterogenous". Hence the "plurally responsive citizen" (Dake and Thompson 1999).

The Rudiments of Cultural Theory

"They will never agree", said the 19th century wit, the Reverend Sidney Smith, when he saw two women shouting at each other from houses on opposite sides of an Edinburgh street, "They are arguing from different premises". Cultural theorists (e.g. Douglas and Wildavsky 1982: 174 and Adams 1995: 50) like to use this story as a way of getting to grips with the "contradictory certainties" that underlie policy disputes such as those around pension reform and sustainable development. The different premises, in these sorts of disputes, concern human and physical nature, and cultural theory maps them in terms of a fivefold typology of forms of social solidarity. (See Figure 2.1. For ease of exposition, I have left one of these forms - it is characterised by withdrawal from social involvement - until later in this chapter.)

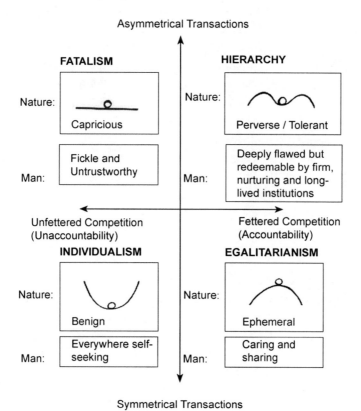

Figure 2.1: Four of The Five Forms Of Social Solidarity And Their Associated Premises (or Myths of Nature)

Two of these solidarities - individualism and hierarchy - have long been familiar to social scientists; they are usually referred to as *markets* and *hierarchies* (e.g. Williamson 1975 and Lindblom 1977).[20] Cultural theory's novelty lies in its addition of the other three forms of solidarity and in its making explicit the different premises - the different social constructions of nature, physical and human - that sustain these five fundamental arrangements for the promotion of social transactions. A concomitant novelty (the implications of which will be a major theme in the remaining chapters of this book) is that, in going from social science's conventional dualisms to cultural theory's fivefold dynamical scheme (though I have not really introduced the dynamics yet), we are going from *simplicity* to *complexity*, in the technical senses of those terms.

Hierarchies institute status differences (asymmetrical transactions, as in the Guards officer explaining "I'd expect to be invited to my sergeant's wedding but he would not expect to be invited to mine") and, by requiring forms of behaviour appropriate to those of differing rank and station (accountability, as in the newspaper headline, after the death of Princess Di, "The Queen Bows To Her People"),[21] set all sorts of limits on competition. Markets - the transactional arrangements that accompany individualism - do the diametrical opposite; they institute equality of opportunity (symmetrical transactions, as in "You scratch my back, I'll scratch yours") and promote competition (no accountability, as in "If I don't do it, someone else will"). The other two permutations: symmetrical transactions with accountability (labelled egalitarianism in the cultural theory scheme), and asymmetrical transactions without accountability (labelled fatalism in the cultural theory scheme) tend to be ignored by social science in general and by policy science in particular.

This, for instance, was evidently the case with the enormous Brent Spar oil storage structure, the deep ocean disposal of which was proposed

---

20　For a more extensive treatment of these dualistic institutional schemes, along with the more recent shifts towards threefold and even fourfold formulations, see Thompson, Verweij and Ellis (2006).

21　"Her people" had become increasingly concerned that there was no flag flying at half-mast on Buckingham Palace, and were not satisfied with the explanation that this was because the Queen was at Balmoral and the royal standard was only flown when she was in residence. The "bow" came when this explanation was discarded and a flag, at half-mast, was flown on the unoccupied palace.

by the market actor, Shell, and approved by the hierarchical actor, the British government's regulatory agency. Had there been only markets and hierarchies the Brent Spar would now be mouldering in its watery grave, but of course it isn't! Another actor, Greenpeace, from a third form of solidarity (egalitarianism) forced its way in, at the 11th hour, by audaciously and very publicly landing a helicopter on the structure as it was being towed out into the Atlantic. The disposal plans were abruptly abandoned by Shell (motorists, particularly in Germany, having stopped buying its petrol) and the British government was left with egg all over its face (John Major, the prime minister at the time, called Shell's senior management "wimps"). Shell then entered into lengthy negotiations with Greenpeace, and the Brent Spar has now been cut up into cylindrical sections to help form a ferry terminal in Norway. Those British citizens who managed to remain ignorant of the whole affair (and they were many), or who found themselves totally convinced by whoever they happened to have last seen arguing their case on television, were evidently bound into none of these "active" solidarities - individualism, hierarchy or egalitarianism - and constituted a fourth and rather "inactive" solidarity - fatalism - assuring one another either that "ignorance is bliss" or that "nothing we could do would make any difference anyway".

□ For upholders of the individualist solidarity, nature is benign - able to recover from any exploitation (hence the iconic myth of nature, illustrated in Figure 2.1: a ball that, no matter how profoundly disturbed, always returns to stability) - and man is inherently self-seeking and atomistic (i.e. the way the methodological individualists assume man is). Trial and error, in self-organising ego-focused networks (markets), is the way to go, with Adam Smith's invisible hand ensuring that people only do well when others also benefit. Individualists, in consequence, trust others until they give them reason not to and then retaliate in kind (the winning "tit for tat" strategy in the iterated Prisoner's Dilemma game [Rapoport 1985]). They see it as only fair that (as in the joint stock company) those who put most in get most out. Managing institutions that work "with the grain of the market" (getting rid of environmentally harmful subsidies, for instance) are what are needed.

☐ Nature, for those who bind themselves into the egalitarian solidarity, is almost the exact opposite (hence the ball on the upturned basin) - fragile, intricately interconnected and ephemeral - and man is essentially caring and sharing (until corrupted by coercive and inegalitarian institutions: markets and hierarchies). We must all tread lightly on the Earth, and it is not enough that people start off equal; they must end up equal as well - equality of result. Trust and levelling go hand-in-hand, and institutions that distribute unequally are distrusted. Voluntary simplicity is the only solution to our environmental problems, with the "precautionary principle" being strictly enforced on those who are tempted not to share the simple life.

☐ The world, in the hierarchical solidarity, is controllable. Nature is stable until pushed beyond discoverable limits (hence the two humps), and man is malleable: deeply flawed but redeemable by firm, long-lasting and trustworthy institutions (i.e. the way the methodological collectivists assume man is, as in "Give me the boy and I will give you the man"). Fair distribution is by rank and station or, in the modern context, by need (with the level of need being determined by expert and dispassionate authority). Environmental management requires certified experts (to determine the precise locations of nature's limits) and statutory regulation (to ensure that all economic activity is then kept within those limits).

☐ Fatalist actors (or perhaps we should say non-actors, since their voice is seldom heard in policy debates; if it was they wouldn't be fatalistic!) find neither rhyme nor reason in nature, and know that man is fickle and untrustworthy. Fairness, in consequence, is not to be found in this life, and there is no possibility of effecting change for the better. "Defect first" - the winning strategy in the one-off Prisoner's Dilemma - makes sense here, given the unreliability of communication and the permanent absence of prior acts of good faith. With no way of ever getting in sync with nature (push the ball this way or that and the feedback is everywhere the same), or of building trust with others, the fatalist's world (unlike those of the other three solidarities) is one in which learning is impossible. "Why bother?", therefore, is the rational management response.

These solidarities, in varying strengths and patterns of pairwise alliance, are clearly discernible almost anywhere you care to look: in debates over water engineering in South Asia (Gyawali 2001); in the international fora where delegates struggle to do something about climate change (Thompson, Rayner and Ney 1998; Verweij 2001); in the different ways international regimes cope with trans-boundary risks such as water pollution (Verweij 2000) and municipalities go about the business of transport planning (Hendriks 1994); in the various ways households set about making ends meet (Dake and Thompson 1999); in the different diagnoses of the pensions crisis in countries with ageing populations (Ney 1997); and in the different panaceas that are variously championed and rejected by theorists of public administration (Hood 1998), to mention but a few.

In all these examples we find that each solidarity, in creating a context that is shaped by its distinctive premises, generates a storyline that inevitably contradicts those that are generated by the other solidarities. Yet, since each distils certain elements of experience and wisdom that are missed by the others, and since each provides a clear expression of the way in which a significant portion of the populace feels we should live with one another and with nature, it is important that they all be taken into some sort of account in the policy process. That, in essence, is the case for clumsiness: the case that I have tried to be persuasive about in the previous chapter.

*   *   *

It is at this point that cultural theory is in danger of becoming the victim of its own success. If it makes sense of so much - much of which, moreover, is not made sense of by other theories - then people are going to demand to know *why* it works so well. In other words, where does this typology *come from*? It can't just be *there*! Something must be keeping it there, in much the same way that the endless and turbulent flow of a river can keep a number of eddies in place on its surface. The challenge, in other words is to explain the dynamics that underlie the cultural theory typology. Only if we can do that can we claim to have a proper theory.[22]

Beyond (or, Rather, Beneath) the Typology

A quick recapitulation of the argument so far - a recapitulation, moreover, that brings in the fifth solidarity - is a sensible first step on the way to this proper theory, and it can be set out in the form of five crucial observations. All five are to do with what is involved in going from the classic markets-and-hierarchies distinction to the cultural theory scheme with its five "eddies": its five recurrent regularities within an endless transactional flux.

"Economic incentives and (or, perhaps, versus) social sanctions" is one way of explaining the markets-and-hierarchies framing. Hierarchies enforce the law of contract, without which markets would not work, and they also do other vital things (such as repelling enemies); markets then get on with the wealth-creating process of innovating, bidding and bargaining. Each, we can see, needs the other, though of course there is always considerable disagreement about just where the line between these two transactional realms should be drawn - most famously, perhaps, in the titanic struggle, in the first half of the last century, between Keynes and Hayek. Keynes wanted a major role for hierarchy; Hayek saw that as "The Road To Serfdom" (Hayek 1944) and wanted the line pushed back as far as it would go. Either way, as Keynes pointed out, a line has to be drawn, thereby winning on points, as it were ("Game, set and match", in the estimation of his most recent biographer [Skidelski 2000 p285]).

The same sort of uneasy symbiosis is evident in what is called "the new institutional economics" (which, since it goes back to Williamson's 1975 book, is really quite long in the tooth: a bit like Oxford's New College, which was new in the fourteenth century). In this framing, spiralling transaction costs (as changing technology, for instance, renders quality control more difficult and expensive) lead to market failure and to the hierarchy having to step in to set prices; and, conversely, markets taking

---

22   It is worth noting that, if we take this as the characterisation of a proper theory, then there are precious few of them in social science.

over when transaction costs fall (as, for instance, they recently have - to almost zero - on the Internet). Each of these ways of organising, moreover, is seen as promoting a distinctive rationality - *procedural* and *substantive* as they are sometimes called: hierarchies being primarily concerned with propriety ("Who has the right to do what and to whom?"); markets being much more outcome-focused ("The bottom line"). In this way, each rationality legitimises one of these ways of organising and, in so doing, renders it viable in an environment that contains the other.

Cultural theory does not reject this classic distinction, but it does add the following crucial observations:

1. You cannot have hierarchies without *hierarchists*, nor markets without *individualists*. That is, the organisational requirements of the whole - the pattern of relationships - must somehow be internalised by the parts. The pattern-making, in other words, goes both ways - from the whole to the parts and from the parts to the whole - and this goes on in such a way as to strengthen that pattern and differentiate it from the other patterns. In this way (and like the chicken and the egg) each becomes the cause of the other: we create the patterns and the patterns create us. Individuality, in consequence, is not within each of us but between us: the individual, in Jon Elster's memorable phrase, is *inherently relational*.[23]

2. If two rationalities are justifiable, as they obviously are here, then the upholders of those rationalities will have to have different convictions as to how the world is and people are: different social constructions of nature, physical and human. Otherwise they could not justify their different actions as being self-evidently sensible and moral, the world and people being the way each of them insists they are. And, for *contradictory*

---

23 "Many properties of individuals ... are inherently relational, so that an accurate description of one individual may involve reference to others." (Elster 1985: 6). Change Elster's "may" to "must" and you have the founding assumption for our anti-dualist approach. Elster is perhaps the leading proponent of methodological individualism and, as Gunnar Grendstad (1994 p26) has pointed out, seems not to have noticed that, in insisting on the inherent relationality of the individual, he has "shot himself in the foot". (This verdict is from an early draft of Grendstad's PhD thesis. The final version reads "flaws his research program".)

certainties such as these to persist, there must always be sufficient uncertainty as to how the world, and the people in it, really are.

3. Since markets institute equality (of opportunity) and promote competition whilst hierarchies institute inequality (status differences) and restrain competition, there are two discriminators at work here. A full typology, therefore, should contain the other two permutations: equality without competition (*egalitarianism*) and inequality with competition (*fatalism*).

4. Since it is possible to contemplate both hierarchies and markets without having to be convinced that either's version - of how the world is and people are - is true, and since the same holds for egalitarianism and fatalism, there may well be a fifth way of organising (it is called *autonomy*) that is stabilized by the deliberate avoidance of the sorts of coercive involvement that are entailed in the other four. However, *hermits* (as the upholders of autonomy have been dubbed)[24] do not transcend the social sphere, because they stabilize their distinctive way of organising in contradistinction to the others. If the four "socially engaged" forms of solidarity were not there the autonomous life would not be liveable. The objection - "four permutations and five solidarities" - recedes once we realise that the cross-over point of our two discriminators corresponds to a rather strange "all-zero" permutation (this will become clearer in the next chapter when these discriminators are re-cast, more correctly, as a transaction matrix).

5. Though each pattern is made up of individuals and their transactions, we should not assume that *an* individual is part of only one pattern. Indeed, as Lockhart (1997) has pointed out, people who strive to keep all their transactions on just

---

24 Since western hermitude has often become snarled up with a distaste for one's fellow humans, a corrective glance eastwards may be helpful here. Himalayan hermits are a convivial lot, and you can usually count on a warm welcome at their caves. It is only when the visitor tries to exert coercion - tries to draw his host into his preferred pattern of social relations - that the atmosphere becomes frosty.

one pattern are hard to live with - we call them fanatics![25] In general, if transactional spheres - workplace and home, for instance - are fairly separate then an individual may lead different parts of his or her life in different patterns.[26] Just because we are physiologically indivisible it does not follow that we are socially indivisible; hence the need to think in terms of *the dividual*, and to take the form of social solidarity (the pattern together with its viability conditions) as the unit of analysis, not the individual.

These, then, are the barest bones of cultural theory. In the chapters that follow I will try to put some dynamic flesh on these bones (particularly on the fifth bone - the form of solidarity as the unit of analysis) and I will try to do this in a way that will make sense to students of institutions: no easy task, given my anti-dualistic and unobvious starting point. But cultural theory does have one thing in its favour: its even-handedness. Where students of institutions have long been faced with a stark choice - methodological individualism or methodological collectivism - cultural theory offers a welcome, and perhaps surprising, escape route: "a plague on both your methodologies!"

---

25 A nice definition, in that it gives us five *kinds* of fanaticism. We can all probably recognise among our acquaintances people who are fanatically inclined to one or other of the three "active" solidarities; Fanatical fatalists and fanatical hermits are more of a problem.

26 The idea of separate "pots", with different sets of rules for putting-in and taking-out (allocative systems, as they are called) may be helpful here. An employer, for instance, is not entitled to dip into the pockets of those he employs (which, of course, is what the disgraced businessman Robert Maxwell did when he raided his company's pension fund) nor should an employee "get his fingers stuck in the till".

CHAPTER 3

Solidarities: the Units of Analysis

Hierarchies are made up of strongly bounded groups - horses, men, officers, in the case of the cavalry regiment in which I spent my formative years - which, of course, limits competition between individuals who are in different groups. I remember a temperamentally rather unhierarchical major being bitten by his horse and promptly biting it back, much to its surprise. Symmetrical behaviour such as this *within* any of the ranked groups was okay, but not *between* them. Indeed, so out-of-line was this behaviour that the story was still being recounted, among both men and officers (and, for all I know, horses too), decades later.[27] But not all strongly bounded groups are hierarchical. Most activist environmental groups, for instance, vehemently reject the inequalities of the hierarchy, and they are also emphatically opposed to what they see as the selfishness of the market and to all the "false needs" that it gives rise to. Earth First!, for instance, puts it like this:

> *To avoid co-option, we feel it is necessary to avoid the corporate organisational structure so readily embraced by many environmental groups. Earth First! is a movement, not an organisation. Our structure is non-hierarchical. We have no highly paid "professional staff" or formal leadership.*[28]

The upholders of the egalitarian solidarity prefer an explicitly levelled and co-operative way of life, and this means that their tightly bounded groups, unlike those that constitute the hierarchy, do not enter into ranked relationships with one another. Where hierarchists are endlessly concerned with proprieties - who has the right to do what and to whom - egalitarians sustain their intense communality by joining together in an

---

27 The horse, I should explain, was a polo pony, the regiment having given up fighting on horses and converted to armoured cars just a few years before the start of the Second World War. Hippophilia and equestrian prowess, however, continued unabated.

28 From the Earth First! website http://www.earthfirstjournal.org/back_issues.php (26 July 2002).

unrelenting and strident criticism of what is going on outside their "wall of virtue". In contrast to the hierarchical solidarity with its procedural rationality, the upholders of egalitarianism cleave to a *critical rationality* (see Figure 3.1) in which the inequities of the market and the hierarchy (and, in particular, their treatment of Mother Nature) provide them with the institutional glue that holds them together. Again, Earth First! say it beautifully:

> *... our activities [by which they mean the activities of all those who are not within the wall of virtue] are now beginning to have fundamental, systemic effects upon the entire life-support system of the planet - upsetting the world's climate, poisoning the oceans, destroying the ozone layer which protects us from ultraviolet radiation, changing the CO_2 ratio in the atmosphere, and spreading acid rain, radioactive fallout, pesticides and industrial contamination throughout the biosphere.*

Radical change now, before it is too late, is thus imperative: a solution so uncompromising as to render that proffered by the hierarchical solidarity - a much more gradual "wise guidance" or "global stewardship" - part of the problem:

> *We - this generation of humans - are at our most important juncture since we came out of the trees six million years ago. It is our decision, ours today, whether Earth continues to be a marvellously living, diverse oasis in the blackness of space, or whether the charismatic megafauna of the future will consist of Norway rats and cockroaches.*[29]

---

29   Some wags, who clearly are on the other side of the wall of virtue, would add "and Keith Richards".

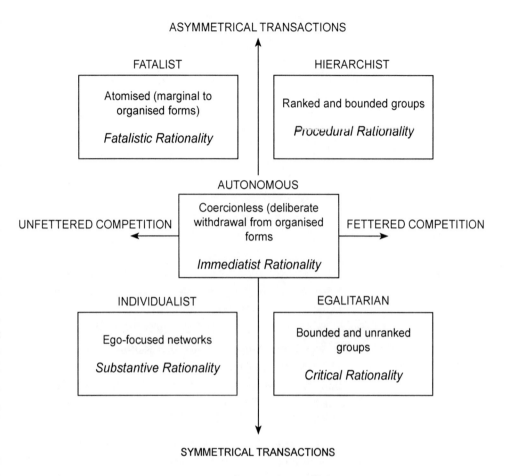

ASYMMETRICAL TRANSACTIONS

FATALIST

Atomised (marginal to organised forms)

Fatalistic Rationality

HIERARCHIST

Ranked and bounded groups

Procedural Rationality

AUTONOMOUS

Coercionless (deliberate withdrawal from organised forms

Immediatist Rationality

UNFETTERED COMPETITION

FETTERED COMPETITION

INDIVIDUALIST

Ego-focused networks

Substantive Rationality

EGALITARIAN

Bounded and unranked groups

Critical Rationality

SYMMETRICAL TRANSACTIONS

Note: The centre of this diagram depicts zero transactions. Transactions increase as one moves away from the centre and the arrows depict the discriminators, in terms of pairs of which these transactions can become patterned.

Figure 3.1: The Five Forms of Solidarity

Similarly, when we turn to the two "ungrouped" forms of solidarity - the individualist and the fatalist - we find that they too have their distinctive rationalities. The "bottom line", not the niceties of status, is what the upholder of individualism cares about, and it is this pragmatic and *substantive rationality* that sustains his market-centred way of life (see Figure 3.1). But by no means all of those who are "ungrouped" (and therefore beyond the reach of the transactional constraints that accompany the hierarchical and egalitarian forms of solidarity) can be characterised as untrammelled entrepreneurs, freely bidding and bargaining on a one-to-one basis with other similarly situated dividuals. To be a fully paid-up member of the "enterprise culture" it is not enough to be free of group constraints; you must also have an extensive personal network. Markets, cultural theory points out, are made up, not of atomised individuals, but of people and their networks.[30] And if you do not have a personal network - which, of course, is the fatalist's predicament - then you cannot join in the market way of life.

To recapitulate a rather complicated (or, at any rate, unfamiliar) argument, cultural theory identifies three patterns of social relationships: three distinctly different ways of organising. These are: the bounded and ranked groups of the hierarchist, the bounded and unranked groups of the egalitarian, and the ego-focused networks of the individualist. But that is not all. As any dressmaker will tell you, you cannot create patterns without creating discards. Those who find themselves on the outside of all three of these patterns (because they cannot conform to the rights and obligations of the hierarchy, cannot muster the communal fervour and commitment of the egalitarian group, and cannot scrape together the entry fee for the market) constitute a fourth solidarity: one in which the decisions that shape the lives of its members are made for them by those who belong to the other three. These are the people whose lives the novelist Mrs Gaskell described as being "like a lottery": the world does things to them - sometimes pleasant, sometimes unpleasant - but nothing they do makes much difference. *Fatalistic resignation* is the only rational response to this sort of predicament (see Figure 3.1).

What About The Hermit: The Upholder of Autonomy?

An awareness that "nothing succeeds like success" is what drives the individualist to enter and, if need be, re-enter the market. An awareness that "nothing makes much difference" reconciles the fatalist to his exclusion. "Each counts as one and no-one more than one" is the promise

---

30 A market, if you think about it, is a group of networks; in contrast to a hierarchy, which is a network of groups (though usually drawn with its central node as the tip of an organisational pyramid). I will have much more to say about these patterns in Chapter 5.

that keeps the egalitarian committed and levelled. The hierarchist, for her part, is more likely to contrast the advantages we all enjoy when the cobbler sticks to his last with the wasteful confusion of keeping a dog and then barking yourself.

That each of these proverbial justifications works for the person who voices it suggests what cultural theory predicts: that you will come to know what you want, and get more of it, by moving in the direction indicated by the proverb.[31] And, since each proverb indicates a different direction, we must be dealing with something that has what students of dynamical systems call *multiple attractors*: the further you go in each of these four directions the more you get of what that direction tells you you want. Yet, for all their differences, these four directions do have one thing in common.

As you move in any of these four directions, as well as getting more of what you want, you also get more and more involved in coercive social relations: more followers (in return for promised rewards) if you're an individualist, more excluded if you're a fatalist, more rights and obligations if you're a hierarchist, and more and more like everyone else if you're an egalitarian. It is possible, however, to become disenchanted with coercion: to want less and less, not more and more, of these diverse satisfactions. In that case you will be behaving rationally if you do the opposite to what all these proverbs tell you to do: that is, if you move back towards a sort of "absolute zero" - a point where transactions, far from being maximised, are minimised. This, of course, is what the hermit does.

The prospect of "heavy scenes" deters the hermit from moving in the "grouped" direction; the awareness that "in getting and spending we lay waste our lives" ensures that he does not career headlong towards the "ungrouped" solidarities. To fully understand how the hermit manages to avoid these twin pitfalls we need to consider something that is not easily grasped: the *social construction of time*. Each of the three patterned

---

31 But does it make sense to speak of the fatalist "wanting" and "getting more of" what he or she wants? "Understanding how things are" and "learning the pointlessness of the behaviours that are latched onto by those who comprise the more active solidarities" better describe the fatalist's journey towards the fatalist attractor.

solidarities projects its distinctive time structure out into the future, so as to ensure that the promises it makes to its constituent individuals are delivered, and seen to be delivered. The promises they make, of course, are different - enhanced statuses for the loyal (hierarchy), profits for the skilled and daring (individualism) and ecocatastrophies avoided for those who tread lightly on the Earth (egalitarianism) - but they are all, in their different ways, coercive. Since the avoidance of coercive social relationships is the first essential of the autonomous way of life, the hermit will have to disengage himself from all these time structures if he is to stabilise his life around the things *he* prefers. Small wonder, then, that he opts for a *rationality of immediacy* (see Figure 3.1), taking no thought for the morrow and considering, instead, the lilies of the field.

Hermits, it is worth pointing out, can be found in some unlikely places. Keynes, for instance, though professionally engaged (in the Treasury, throughout the Second World War) in the challenging business of finding the means by which Nazi Germany could be overcome, managed never to stray far from the autonomous attractor. He was famously dismissive of elaborated time perspectives ("In the long run we are all dead"), saw scarcity as a temporary phenomenon (a blip caused by "the economics of industrialism") and remained confident that, very soon, we would not need to bother even about the short term.

> ...*we shall once more value ends above means and prefer the good to the useful. We shall honour those who can teach us how to pluck the hour and the day virtuously and well, the delightful people who are capable of taking direct enjoyment in things, the lilies of the field who toil not neither do they spin.*
> [Keynes as quoted by Skidelsky (2000: p478).]

The Impossibility Theorem

"Why five?", "Why these five?", "Why not any of a hundred other solidarities and their justifying proverbs?" are the objections that are provoked by this cultural theory diagram. And then there is the question of their co-existence: "If they're all in competition for adherents how come one of them doesn't win and extinguish all the others?" The feeling, even among those who are less than satisfied with the conventional markets-

and-hierarchies account, is that this fivefold scheme, with its selected proverbs and its special pleadings, has to be the most preposterous thing ever to come down the pike.

Well, it just so happens that cultural theory's impossibility theorem - that there are these five and just these five - has been proved. Indeed, as sometimes happens with theorems, it was proved before it was stated. Back in 1980, two mathematically-minded sociologists, Manfred Schmutzer and Wyllis Bandler, expressed the process by which relationships can be built up into patterns (or "organisations", as they called them) in terms of a "transaction matrix" which, they showed, can be solved only if certain conditions are met. They framed these conditions in terms of two cybernetic notions: *openness*, which corresponds to cultural theory's "unfettered competition", and *strong connectedness*, which corresponds to cultural theory's "symmetrical transactions" (see Figure 3.1). There are, in all, just four solutions:

1. When there is openness and strong connectedness the solution corresponds to the ego-focused networks that characterise market relationships.

2. When there is closure and weak connectedness the matrix can be rearranged to be "upper triangular", which means that all relationships are hierarchically organised ("asymmetrical" in cultural theory terms).

3. When there is closure and strong connectedness we get what is technically an "insoluble matrix". It is insoluble because, instead of giving an across-the-board pattern (an "organisation" in Schmutzer and Bandler's terms), it results in a number of separate polka dots. The members of each dot are strongly connected to one another but each dot is so closed that there are no connections from any member of one dot to any member of any of the other dots.

4. There is a seemingly trivial solution where you cannot really speak of either condition. This is when the matrix transforms into what is called an "all-zero matrix". Not open and not closed (neither unfettered nor fettered in cultural theory terms),

not strongly connected and not weakly connected (neither symmetrical nor asymmetrical in cultural theory terms), this solution is at the absolute zero: no transactions between any individuals.

Schmutzer and Bandler (1980) knew they had proved *something* but, until cultural theory's impossibility theorem was stated (Thompson, Ellis and Wildavsky, 1990), they did not know what! Now, however, they are satisfied that their four solutions fit the individualist, the hierarchist, the egalitarian and the hermit respectively. The remaining permutation (open but weakly connected) which, they had proved, has no solution, fits the fatalist: no organisation and no pattern. Schmutzer and Bandler (1991, personal communication) point out that these five outcomes (which, their proof makes clear, are all the outcomes there are) are "truly distinct types that cannot be transformed into each other unless the principal conditions are altered".[32]

This - the impossibility theorem - formally establishes the first half of cultural theory: that there are just these five solidarities: just these five ways in which relationships can be arranged into patterns that are viable. The second half is concerned with explaining why, even though they are in endless competition for adherents, no one of these solidarities ever goes into permanent extinction. The argument here is that each of these solidarities is only viable in an environment that contains the others. This gives us the "requisite variety condition": that if one solidarity is there they will all be there.

The Requisite Variety Condition

Schmutzer and Bandler's five outcomes are "pure types", in that everyone becomes organised in the same way: one pattern, as it were, drives out all the others. Since they were concerned only with proving how many patterns there can be, Schmutzer and Bandler did not need to consider

---

32   A more recent exposition of this proof is to be found in Schmutzer (1994).

whether such pure types are socially possible. Cultural theory, of course, says they are not (and, though this has not yet been proved, it has been demonstrated by computer simulation [Thompson and Tayler, 1985]).[33]

The basic idea is that each way of organising ultimately *needs* the others, because they do something vital for it that it could never do for itself. Indeed, this sort of dependency does not have to be mutual; it is enough if each way does something vital for just one of the others and no one of them is left out. If that condition is satisfied then the solidarities will arrange themselves into what students of self-organising systems call a *hypercycle*: like that party game where each child is supported on the knees of the child behind. One reviewer of *Cultural Theory*, Barry Schwartz (1991 p765), has nicely summarised this state of affairs, and its consequences for the sorts of social changes that students of institutional behaviour would so dearly like to understand.

> ... *each way of life, unchecked, undermines itself. Individualism would mean chaos without hierarchical authority to enforce contracts and repel enemies. To get work done and settle disputes the egalitarian order needs hierarchy too. Hierarchies, in turn, would be stagnant without the creative energy of individualism, incohesive without the binding force of equality, unstable without the passivity and acquiescence of fatalism. Dominant and subordinate ways of life thus exist in alliance. Yet this relationship is fragile, constantly shifting, constantly generating a societal environment conducive to change.*

In summary, we can say that cultural theory's overall picture is of a fivefold self-organising system in which transactions are being maximised (or, in the fatalist's case, imposed and, in the hermit's case, minimised) without at the same time destroying the cognitive means by which those who are busy organising themselves this way or that are able to experience, and

---

33   This demonstration consists of a highly stylised agent-based (ie "bottom up") model: 30 "firms", each of which has to latch onto one or other of the strategies appropriate to the four solidarities (we left out the autonomous solidarity) with the aim of prospering in its environment, which is simply the other firms and their various strategies, and it turns out that only when all four are available does the game exhibit "lifelike" behaviour: economic upswings, downswings, shake-outs and so on.

hence prefer and promote, their different ways of organising. Groups and networks, separately or in combination (a hierarchy, for instance, is a network of groups), as the impossibility theorem shows, provide the vital patterns - the multiple attractors - for all this self-organisation. But it is not the patterns that organise the people, even though the people do end up organised into those patterns. If anything, it is the other way round. In seeking to make sense out of their lives (that is, in discovering their preferences), people inevitably organise themselves into the patterns that enable them to do this. Cultural theory's aim is to explain those patterns and the processes by which they are sustained and transformed.

What's New About That?

The process by which people simultaneously transact with one another and make sense out of what they are doing, of course, is not something that lay undiscovered until cultural theory came along. It has long been a focus of attention, and one well-elaborated theory - *transaction theory* - is concerned with little else. Transaction theory, unlike so much of social science, does not take culture - the shared beliefs and values that justify behaviour - as given. Its intellectual heart, therefore, is in much the same place as cultural theory's. But how do they fit together?

Fredrik Barth (in his classic paper, "Models of Social Organisation", 1966) sets out to provide an answer to the big question that is ducked by so much of social science: how do people who act in their interest come to *know* where that interest lies? He begins (as does cultural theory) with the idea that a person, initially, does not really know what he wants. Uninvolved with others, he has a rag-bag of disparate values and, on the basis of these values, he enters into transactions over objects that both he and those he transacts with happen to value. His rag-bag of values provides him with a way of seeing the world and, thanks to that, he is able to discern what courses of action are available to him.[34] He is also

---

34 The objection - that Barth seems to be explaining how people get their preferences by assuming that they set off with some of them already in place - has been rebutted by Robert Heiner (1983). Heiner uses simple mathematical arguments to show that, faced with an uncertain environment, it is advantageous ("rational" as Herbert Simon would say) to limit your choice of actions. That way, you stand a chance of learning *something* about the world: an insight that is consistent with Barth's "rag-bag assumption", and which is now routinely adopted by modellers of artificial life.

able to predict their likely outcomes and hence to select the course that he assesses to be the most advantageous. Since those with whom he is transacting are likely to have rather differently constituted rag-bags, the chances are that there will be a mismatch between what he expects to happen and what actually happens. In the light of this mismatch, he can then re-arrange his values in the hope of doing rather better next time. The end result of this rational behaviour, across myriad and often overlapping transactions, is that his rag-bag of values gradually becomes more systematized, more internally consistent and more like those of the people with whom he transacts.

This model of the transactional process exactly matches the cultural theory argument that as you move away from the centre of the diagram (see Figure 3.1), in any of the four directions, you will simultaneously come to know more clearly what you want, get more and more of it, and become more and more involved with others.[35] The one big difference is that transaction theory has no directions. It simply has this systematizing, integrating and homogenizing process, and the idea is that we all follow it: we start off all over the place and we all end up at the same place. Cultural theory, by contrast, argues that there are five places, each of which *emerges* once the transacting starts, and that some of us end up at each of them. Of course, we do not all stay where we end up - there is always some movement of people between these places (and I will come to that in a later chapter) - but social life is absolutely not a one-way journey to a single destination.

Transaction theory, therefore, has confused the local dynamic - the homing-in process - with the global outcome: the five solidarities (see Figure 3.2). It has assumed that, because we all home-in on something, there is only one something there for us all to home-in on. Extricating social science from that self-inflicted dead-end, you could say, is what cultural theory is all about.

---

35   Actually it is not quite as simple as this, because the centre too is an attractor, and it is in moving towards this that the hermit learns what he wants and does not want. To represent all this correctly we need a diagram (Figure 3.2) in which the five attractors are made explicit.

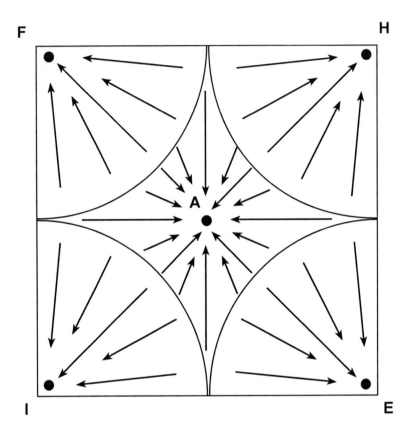

Figure 3.2: The five attractors and their separatrices (the "watersheds" between the attractors)

Five Destinations

I would not want to give the impression that cultural theory is exclusively the creation of social scientists, nor would I want to give any encouragement to the view that physical and natural scientists need not bother themselves about it. "Against dualism" reads the cultural theory banner, and the neat separation of facts and values is one of its prime targets. Though the followers of the different ways of life may all agree on certain "nursery facts", such as that water does not flow uphill, there is much on which they do not agree.[36]

In all those situations where the true state of the world is not entirely certain (global warming, for instance, or the health effects of low-level radiation, or the risks from "mad cow disease", or the future of fusion energy, to mention but a few) the upholders of each form of solidarity tend to choose those possible states of the world that best support their way of organising and most discomfort those of their rivals. These "social constructions of reality" are so predictable, so enduring, and so directly translated into divergent behaviours, that they were first described, not by social scientists, but by ecologists.

Ecologists who study *managed* eco-systems - grasslands, for instance, forests and fisheries - encounter the institutions that are doing the managing, not as organised inputs to some decision making process, but as physical interventions in the eco-systems they are studying. What they found was that, even when the initial conditions were identical, the interventions were not. For instance, some Canadian managers had started spraying the forest with insecticide, others had stopped. But they didn't do just anything: there *was* a consistent pattern to their diverse interventions. The problem the ecologists faced was this: if the managers were irrational there would be no discernible patterns in what they did; if they were rational they would all do the same. The ecologists' elegant, and eminently scientific, solution was to ask themselves this question: what are the minimal representations of reality that will have to be ascribed to each managing institution if it is to be granted the dignity of rationality?

---

36 Brian Wynne has taken me to task on this, pointing out that there are many situations in which water *does* flow uphill: capillary action, for instance. Well, yes, but we can all agree on the explanations for those exceptions. Agreement such as that, however, is lacking when we come to something like the Brent Spar oil storage structure. For Shell there were no risks associated with its ocean disposal. For the UK government scientists disposal was safe only within certain limits, for Greenpeace there were no safe limits.

They found that they needed at least three representations - which they called *myths of nature* - each of which could be expressed as a little picture of a ball in a landscape (Holling, 1986; Holling, Gunderson and Peterson, 1993). All that was left for the social scientist to do (as, of course, I have just been doing) was to show how each of these pictures rationalises just one of the five solidarities, and to fill in the two missing myths: the fatalist's and the hermit's.[37] (See Figure 3.3.)

Myths, Holling et al are careful to point out, are not falsehoods. Each myth captures some essence of experience and wisdom, and there is ample scientific evidence for the world (at times and in places) being each of these four ways. There is also ample evidence for the validity of the hermit's myth - *nature resilient*.

The essence of experience and wisdom that is captured by the hermit's myth (and missed by the other four) is the *transformational* nature of ball and landscape: the fact that the movement of the ball alters the landscape through which it moves. If we imagine that the ball is imbued with "anti-gravity", so that it sucks up the landscape as it moves through it, we can represent the hermit's myth as subsuming the other four myths as "stills" in a never-ending cycle of change: benign to perverse/tolerant to capricious to ephemeral and then, as the ball rolls off the upturned basin, to some other benign trough. (See Figure 3.4.)

---

37 These two had been overlooked because hermit and fatalist managers are not commonly found in those national institutions that strive to control natural resources. More's the pity!

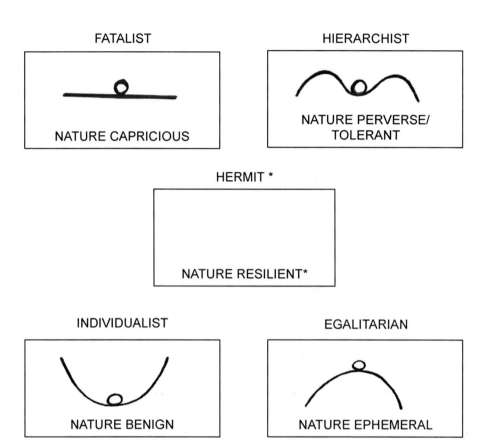

FATALIST

NATURE CAPRICIOUS

HIERARCHIST

NATURE PERVERSE/
TOLERANT

HERMIT *

NATURE RESILIENT*

INDIVIDUALIST

NATURE BENIGN

EGALITARIAN

NATURE EPHEMERAL

* The hermit's myth cannot be represented by a single picture, because it subsumes the other four. (See Figure 3.4)

Figure 3.3: The Five Myths of Nature

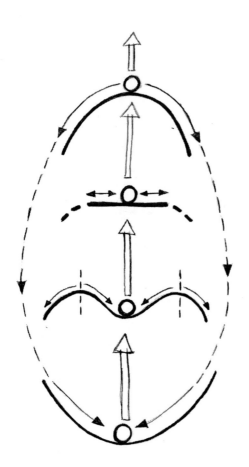

The thicker arrows depict the transformations of the landscape that result from the ball's movement through it. The fine arrows depict the movement of the ball at the key stages of this transformational process.

The broken fine arrows indicate that the basin that marks the start of the next cycle is a different basin.[38]

Figure 3.4: The Hermit's Myth: Nature Resilient

The different behaviours that sustain the five ways of organising are rationalised (and morally justified) by these myths of nature, each of which provides its holders with their distinctive definition of the ends - the needs and the resources - that they must make meet if they are to remain viable.

---

38   Landscapes such as this are quite familiar to geomorphologists and biologists. Biologists call them *epigenetic landscapes*, and geomorphologists need them to explain *relict features*: features in an existing landscape that can only be explained by reference to a previous landscape that is no longer there.

It is at this point that cultural theory diverges (once again) from the mainstream of social science, where the commonsense assumption is that our resources are given to us by physical nature and our needs by human nature. "Not so", say cultural theorists, "needs and resources are socially constructed" (Dake and Thompson, 1993). In other words, the members of each form of solidarity make the ends themselves before they make them meet.

Egalitarians, for instance, speak of "natural resources" whilst individualists speak of "raw materials", those raw materials becoming resources only when human skill, ingenuity and daring have been successfully brought to bear upon them. For egalitarians, therefore, resources are finite - they are what nature has given us (hence the precariousness of our position as we draw upon them). For individualists, however, resources are something we ourselves create out of the "clay" that nature has provided (and there's plenty of that!). Resources, therefore, are limited only by our lack of imagination and our unwillingness to engage in trial-and-error. Of course, if our first experiment were likely to be our last (as it would be if nature were ephemeral, and might be if nature were perverse/tolerant) or if we could never learn anything from our experiments (as would be the case if nature were capricious) we would be in serious trouble. Nature, therefore, *has* to be benign.

Where egalitarians construct for themselves a world of *resource depletion* (a Malthusian world in which we must all be frugal and no one should have more of anything than anyone else) and individualists construct a world of *resource abundance* (an Adam Smithian world in which the skilful, the forceful and the lucky benefit everyone by the exuberant pursuit of their self-interest), the hierarchist prefers a world of *resource scarcity*. Hierarchists do want the resource cake to grow bigger, but only when controlled and managed by their certified experts. If the resource cake could not grow (worse still, if it kept getting smaller) hierarchists would find it increasingly difficult to share it out unequally, and they would find it ever more difficult to attract followers to their way of life.[39] On the other hand, if the cake could grow just by unleashing the free-

---

39 But not impossible. In wartime, rationing is usually accepted, with the sacrifices each person must make for the sake of the totality actually strengthening the hierarchical solidarity. But rationing in peacetime is more of a problem.

for-all of individualistic trial-and-error, there would be no need for all the carefully planned procedures, expertises, proper channels, statutory regulations and so on that are the means by which the hierarchical solidarity institutes and reproduces itself. The social construction that sustains the hierarchist, therefore, has a positive-sum pocket beyond which lies trouble: a world in which everything hinges on finding out where the dividing line lies and then making sure that people stay on the right side of it.

The hermit, for his part, has to avoid being taken over by any of these contradictory certitudes, and this he does by conceding that each is true *up to a point*. Since the hermit's myth tells him that the ravening desires each of the other myths incites in its holders only serve to hasten its conquest by the next one in the cycle, his aim in life is to avoid finding himself caught up in this coercive merry-go-round. Desires, he concludes, are fuelled by ignorance and, since ignorance is something he wishes to rid himself of, he eliminates what he sees to be the false dualism inherent in all the other myths - the clear separation of ball and landscape - and thereby makes himself one with nature.

And so it goes, each solidarity supplying its constituent individuals (its *social beings*, as Durkheim would say) with the convictions, the preferences and the moral justifications that will support that solidarity and, at the same time, distance it from its rivals.

*   *   *

Lest it appear that in speaking of social beings (the hermit, the hierarchist and so on) and of solidarities (autonomy, hierarchy and so on) I have fallen victim to the sort of dualistic thinking that I am trying to get rid of, I should point out that social beings and solidarities are just two ways of looking at the same thing. We create the patterns and, since (as even Jon Elster has conceded) the individual is inherently relational, the patterns create us. If we do not embrace the certitudes that come with the myth of nature that supports the pattern of which we are part, and if we do not act rationally in the light of these certitudes, then the pattern will begin to fall apart and we will find ourselves less and less clear as to what our preferences are.[40] This, of course, *can* happen (it is called *anomie*) but not everywhere and not all the time. Social beings and solidarities are not separate, or separable; they constitute one another.

---

40   Not that this requires one hundred percent adherence. *Genericity* - enough conformity, enough of the time, and with the non-conformist behaviour not being consistently patterned according to one or other of the contending solidarities - is all that is needed.

CHAPTER 4

In Praise of Bias

One of the eternal troubles with the study of institutions is the lack of agreement among those who study them as to what institutions *are*. Those who call themselves "the new institutionalists" wish to broaden the definition to take in all those organisational structures and processes whose scope is national or international or industry-wide (Powell and Di Maggio, 1991: p9).[41] Institutional economists working in the area of game theory cast their net even wider and interpret the equilibria in repeated games as institutions (Ostrom, 1990; Sugden, 1986). Such games, of course, can encompass just a few individuals: much less than a nation or an industry.

My own preference is to go the whole hog and say that an institution is any non-randomness in behaviour (or, indeed, in the beliefs and values that are used to justify that behaviour). Now, of course, the game theorists' equilibria are non-randomnesses, and so too are the new institutionalists' large-scale structures and processes, but there are many non-randomnesses that are not caught by these crude and rather arbitrary definitions: the Sherpa habit of not mentioning the names of the dead, for instance. What possible advantage, it might be objected, could the inclusion of this ethnographic oddity, alongside the state, the market and the iterated prisoner's dilemma, bring to our understanding of institutions? Quite a lot, is my reply.

If you do not mention the names of people once they are dead then it will be difficult for you to construct any genealogies. You cannot get far with those sequences of who begat whom if you are restricted to those ancestors who are still alive! So the Sherpas' non-randomness

---

41 Though March and Olsen (1989: p18 and 1995), with their focus on institutions as "the framework within which politics takes place", are most directly concerned with formal organisations such as parliaments, ministries, courts and administrative agencies. So, even among the new institutionalists, we find the defining line being drawn in different places.

as they cross the conversational line between the living and the dead is not just an insignificant cultural idiosyncrasy; it is a clear-cut example of time being socially constructed one possible way rather than another (Thompson, 1982). Honouring the ancestors is an hierarchical preference. By remembering (and, if need be, inventing) their lines of descent, hierarchists anchor their collectivity in the weight of history. Such a course of action, however, would open up vast craters (exclusive, descent-based claims to resources, for instance) all over the playing field that the market individualist goes to such pains to level. And if all his tomorrows were tightly linked to all those glorious yesterdays, what chance would the hermit have of living just for the moment? Solomon in all his glory would win out every time over the shallow-rooted and short-lived lilies of the field!

In other words, non-randomnesses, though they may appear so numerous and so ubiquitous as to benign impossible to handle, are never just any which way. The Sherpa's reluctance to mention the names of the dead meshes nicely with the individualistic exuberance of his trading expeditions down into the plains of India and over onto the plateau of Tibet.[42] And, in his later widower years, it comports with his dignified withdrawal to a cave in the cliff-face above the house he has already passed on to his youngest child. So is there some way in which we can "measure" a non-randomness so as to see which solidarity it goes with and which solidarities it does not go with?

My candidate for this measure is *information rejection*. If the Sherpa is going to achieve his preferred construction of time then he is going to have to reject something - the names of the dead - that is highly-prized information so far as the hierarchist is concerned. Since any non-randomness can be expressed in terms of a line separating information from "noise", the notion of information rejection promises us just the sort of generalised measure that we need if we are to make sense of all the institutions that this broadest of all possible definitions gives us.

---

42 I do not want to give the impression that this individualistic behaviour is an exclusively male preserve. Sherpa women are often successful traders, in which cases the husband (or husbands; Sherpas practise fraternal polyandry) stays at home. See Thompson (1982).

My argument, therefore, is an argument in praise of bias. Bias, I maintain, is to organising as gravity is to walking about: we would be in a bad way without it! Those who are organising one way will draw the line between information and noise in a very different place to those who are organising in other ways, and that line then has to be defended. Information rejection - its varieties and who is doing which to whom - leads us straight into the organisational plurality that characterises all those outfits that we misguidedly call "organisations". Take, for example, an Everest expedition.

When Men And Mountains Meet

Conventional accounts of Everest expeditions locate authority and control at the top, with the expedition leader, and it is indeed true that the leader (and those to whom he delegates) do appear to make most of the decisions. They constitute a formal and visible structure - an *overground leadership*. But the "lowerarchs" - those who find themselves on the receiving end of this overground leadership - do not meekly fall into line. They crystallize out into an information culture - an *underground leadership* - that is not at all the same as that exercised by the executives and middle managers.

For me, the great attraction in studying social and cultural life above 25,000 feet is that, because everything is stressed to the very limit, all sorts of phenomena that tend to remain hidden at sea-level become visible. Two leaderships within a single enterprise, we might suppose, will be a recipe for instability. One, surely, will drive out the other, or else the enterprise itself will split into two. Since neither of these things happened, we are faced with some interesting questions:

☐ How did the leaderships emerge?

☐ How did they operate?

☐ How did they interact?

To answer these questions I will rely on an article I wrote (for a mountaineering magazine, not an academic journal, 1976) immediately after my return from the 1975 expedition to the South West Face of

Everest. [Excerpts from the article itself are in italics. Since it has now been republished several times, the article evidently hit some nail on the head. Indeed I had a letter from Sir Jack Longland, saying that exactly the same leadership dynamics were at work in the pre-war Everest expedition of which he had been a member.]

The Emergence of the Leaderships

Our Leader had decreed that, in order not to place an intolerable burden upon the Nepalese countryside, we should walk to Base Camp in two parties, one travelling a day behind the other. Perhaps unwisely, he labelled these the "A Team" and the "B Team", and immediately there was much speculation as to the underlying basis for his selection. At first, there were fears among the B Team that the choice of summiters had already taken place and that they were travelling with the leader in order that they could plot the fine details of the assault in secrecy. But even the most paranoid could not sustain this belief for long, and a more popular theory was that "the chaps" were in the A Team and "the lads" were in the B Team. This perhaps was nearer the truth, since what had happened was that Chris [Bonington] had, quite understandably, taken with him all the executives: Sirdar Per-Temba, Base Camp Manager Mike Cheney, Equipment Officer Dave Clarke, Senior Doctor Charles Clarke, and of course the media in the shape of the Sunday Times reporter and the television team. These middle managers were, during their two weeks walk, to have the interesting experience of, in the words of Our Leader, "being let in on his thinking". The B Team, gloriously free of logistics, planning scenarios, computer print-outs, communication set-ups and the like, sank into that form of communal warmth generated by squaddies in a barrackroom: that impenetrable bloody-mindedness born of the I-only-work-here mentality of the shop-floor. A series of perfectly sensible decisions led to the emphasis of a division that is always incipiently present in any large expedition. The A Team represented the Overground Leadership, the B Team the Underground Leadership.

Though the division is now undoubtedly there, there is, I would readily concede, little sign of any leadership emanating from the B Team. But of course we are not on the mountain yet!

After two weeks of walking through the foothills, during which they quickly evolved their very different ways of doing things, the A and B teams came together at Base Camp: a miserable tented shanty-town on the Khumbu Glacier, directly below the first serious obstacle: The Icefall.

At this early stage of the climb there were far too many Chiefs and far too many Indians, and this, coupled with the fact that there was only one camp and that all the action took place within full view of it, meant that the traditional avenues whereby the Underground Leadership could assert its devious influence were firmly closed. Even so, the Overground Leadership could be contained, to some extent, by witchcraft accusations, of which the most feared (and therefore most effective) were "secret-eating" and "equipment-hoarding".

On the positive side, once the expedition is strung out over a number of camps and communications are strained, the Underground can influence the course of events by withholding information. In this way the Overground still makes all the decisions, but on the basis of grossly inadequate information, and this means that, skilfully handled, the Overground, without realising it, simply okays the wishes of the Underground. When communications are really stretched it may be possible to ignore the Overground completely and present them with, in Mick Burke's phrase, "a fait accompli, as they say in Spain". For this kind of action to be constructive in the long-run, one needs a leader who changes his mind a lot and has difficulty in remembering from one day to the next what he has decided. We were fortunate in having such a leader.

Both leaderships are now clearly in place and operating, each by its own logic, without displacing the other. But, of course, since they are operating within the same "organism" they are also interacting with one another. How, you might wonder, can that ever be constructive for the whole? To answer this question we will have to move up to 26,500 feet.

Camp 5, perched in its little notch, was filled with slightly unbalanced euphoria. Our Leader, doing his usual thing of shooting up to the front (and rightly so), had now entered his Mad Mahdi phase, running out drums of rope in the wrong direction, ranting on at Ang Phurpa about "really good Sherpa food", working out logistics on his porridge-encrusted electronic calculator, and communicating his befuddled instructions to the outside world on a broken walkie-talkie that had been persuaded to work again by jamming a ball-point pen into its circuitry.

[Also at Camp 5 was Doug Scott, one of the leading lights of the Underground.] A changed man, he explained to me that, at the very moment when success was within our grasp, the impossible had happened: the Underground and the Overground had merged into a single upward-thrusting force. Miraculously free, for the moment, of Sandhurst-trained leaders and trades-unionised bureaucrats, at peace with the world, he could direct his all towards what Don Whillans [the great climbing plumber] would call: "T'job we've come 'ere for". He was his own man at last.

And he was right about the Leaderships. Bonington and his image were now clearly separate, and all the logistics of climbing Everest were condensed into just six heavy loads that just six of us would have to carry through the Rock Band the next day to establish Camp 6. In the jargon of the management scientist, success on Everest requires massive redundancy, duplication and overlap, but this is just what we didn't have. If just one of us didn't make it up the fixed ropes, then the summit bid would be off. What was more, the route through the Rock Band was not complete, nor had a site for Camp 6 been found. Doug and Dougal [Haston] would have to set off before us, complete the route, fix 300 feet of rope, and find and excavate a site for their summit box [a tiny 2-man tent]. In consequence, it was a happy little non-redundant, unduplicated, non-overlapping group that sat enjoying the view

and the sunshine that afternoon in the little crow's nest that was
Camp 6.

Two days later, Doug Scott and Dougal Haston reached the summit and
the South West Face was climbed.

The Inevitability of Subversion

There are some interesting and subtle dynamics at work within this
expedition: dynamics, moreover, that have some serious implications
for theories of leadership and organisation. Perhaps the most important
message in this story is that *subversion is inevitable*. That is, if there
is an Overground then there will be at least one Underground. The
viability of the whole depends on the contradiction of the parts. So I
have trouble with the notion of *an* organisation. The success of this
Everest expedition cannot be accounted for in terms of just a single way
of organising: "Follow my leader and we'll all get to the top". No, it was
the constructive interplay of at least two contending ways of organising
that made the expedition, as a whole, successful.

To put it at its bluntest, we can have no understanding of leadership
and organisation until we have a *typology of rallying points*: that is, a
comprehensive list of information cultures and a specification of the
conditions under which each of them will "crystallize out". Fortunately,
we don't have to build this typology from scratch. Some of it (as I
have mentioned earlier) is already in place: in the classic social science
distinction between *hierarchies* and *markets*.

A Partial Typology of Rallying Points

The Overground Leadership, with its clearly designated offices, its chains
of command, and its non-overlapping spheres of responsibility, fits nearly
into the hierarchy category, and this is confirmed by all the emphases on
procedure, control and communication that gave organisational coherence
to the A Team. The Underground, on the other hand, had none of these
hierarchical features. That is why I have had to describe Doug Scott as
a "leading light": someone who has no official status but who attracts
support purely by the force of his personality and the scale of his upward

momentum. Nor, once the logistics have shrunk to just six rucksacks full of equipment, and the media have been left thousands of feet behind, is it too difficult to see how Bonington came to shed his image and merge his vital contribution with those of the other five inhabitants of Camp 5.

At Camp 5 we are no longer talking planning and procedures; we're talking *networks*: individualistic and successful actors willingly cooperating to achieve something that, to their great regret, no one of them can achieve unaided. But, though hierarchies and markets certainly explain a lot, they do not explain everything. In particular, they do not explain the dynamics: the emergence, the development and the eventual merging of the two leaderships. Nor do they explain all the things that were going on lower down the mountain, among the loyal but disgruntled hierarchists (who felt they had been abandoned by their leader) and among the *prima donnas*: those "star-quality" climbers who saw themselves as summit material but found themselves in the wrong place at the wrong time.

A Complete Typology of Rallying Points

To briefly recapitulate the cultural theory argument that is set out in the previous chapter, hierarchies and markets are distinguished by two independent criteria: inequality/equality[43] and competition-limiting/ competition-promoting. The other two permutations - inequality with unfettered competition, and equality with fettered competition - provide us with the missing solidarities: fatalism and egalitarianism. Fatalism is the odd one out in this expanded typology, because it does not have a pattern of social relationships associated with it. The distinctive feature of fatalism is that its occupants find themselves on the outside of all three patterns: ranked and bounded groups (the hierarchist's pattern), bounded but unranked groups (the egalitarian's "polka dot" pattern) and ego-focused networks (the individualist's pattern). These four "socially engaged" solidarities are then joined by a fifth way - the hermit's - in which transactions are minimised by a deliberate withdrawal from all social involvement.

---

43   More correctly, asymmetry/symmetry of transactions, which then translate into this inequality/equality distinction: a distinction, however that becomes a little clouded when we realise that each solidarity has its own idea of what is equal, what is fair and so on.

An Everest expedition provides a sort of open-air laboratory for the study of these rallying points. It amply demonstrates the inadequacy of the classic two-fold typology, and it shows how much better we can do in explaining what is going on if we bring in the fatalist and egalitarian rallying points. Even so, my analysis is still not quite complete; I have ignored the hermit. Or have I? Is it not possible that I - the story-teller - am the hermit?

From Two Rallying Points to Four

The expedition, clearly, could not even get itself to Base Camp if there was no planning. Hence we have Bonington-the-Staff-Officer, forming his team, securing his financial support and designating all the tasks - food, equipment, Sherpas, medicine, transport and so on - without which there would be no chance of triumphing over this "last great problem" in Himalayan mountaineering. Months later, with the food nearly all eaten, the equipment all distributed and draped across the mountain, the Sherpas merrily gathering together the choicest pieces as their "swag", the aircraft returned to Heathrow and the yaks to their pastures, and the patients killed or cured, there is very little left for the hierarchists to stay loyal to. But it is what is happening (and not happening) *between* these two states of affairs - the ordered beginning and the mad-rush end - that is the key to the expedition's success.

The cultural divergence of the A Team and the B Team is inevitable. The hierarchy, once concentrated into the A Team, simply forces the B Team away from it. If there were only hierarchies and markets then the B Team would end up at the individualist rallying point and that would be the end of the story. But cultural theory shows us that there are other rallying points, besides hierarchy, and the B Team's odyssey is threaded through them all (even, perhaps, the hermit's) with many a slip along the way!

Initially, with no scope available for subversion (constructive or otherwise), the B Team lapses into fatalism. Then, once Base Camp is reached and the climbing starts, they are able to subvert hierarchy by the levelling tactics of witchcraft accusations. This, I need hardly point out, is not consistent with an individualist strategy. Individualists do not go in for the politics of envy; they favour conspicuous personal success -

Dougal Haston, for instance, dancing his way up the Khumbu Icefall in his crampons and flared Levis (it *was* the Seventies!) and completing the route through it days quicker than the computer had said was humanly possible.

In other words, there is a brief and none-too-visible phase in which the Underground makes the crucial transition from fatalism to individualism by way of egalitarianism. After that, provided we stick with the small number of climbers who push on up onto the South-West Face, it is individualism all the way. Elsewhere on the mountain, however, some climbers fall back into fatalism, others stay loyal to the hierarchy (even when there's virtually nothing left to stay loyal to) and yet others separate out into resentful little cliques: the media versus the inconsiderate climbers, for instance, Icefall Sherpas striking against the high-handed behaviour of their employers, and (believe it or not) working-class Scots ganging-up against the perfidious English bourgeoisie. The whole thing, in other words, can lurch in any of four directions, often remarkably quickly, and success (even if the technical difficulties turn out not to be insuperable) is by no means a foregone conclusion.

Again, cultural theory diverges from the sociological mainstream, where the assumption is that institutions are long-lasting, permanent, reassertive, slow-to-change and so on. Cultural theorists, however, insist that institutions are made afresh each morning, all be it often enough (but by no means always) in the same form as they were made yesterday morning.[44] And, with the form of solidarity as the unit of analysis, and with *an* individual often moving in and out of several solidarities in the course of a single day, the sorts of rapid lurches that our Everest climbers make are only to be expected.

So who rallies which way, and how? To answer this question, (and to leave the confines of this Everest expedition so as to address all those other situations for which it provides such an apt parable) we will need to unravel the information cultures: the ways in which information is defined, shared and defended at each of the rallying points. The neatest way of doing this, I have discovered, is by questioning the prevalent

---

44   But this, when it occurs, is something that needs to be explained.

assumption (among information technologists, at any rate) that people want information. In other words, I am now going to focus on *information rejection*.

Styles of Information Rejection[45]

By "information rejection" I mean something much stronger than Herbert Simon's (1978) notion of *bounded rationality*: the idea that people, when taking a decision, do not take everything into account. Nor do I want to equate information rejection with Cyert and Marsh's (1963) observation that our rationality is bounded by the limits that our physiological equipment (our neurological circuits and so on) place on our information-processing abilities. The trouble with both these approaches is that they still leave us with *rationality in the singular*. And, if there is only one of something, then you do not need a typology.

My argument is, first, that people deliberately stop *way short* of these physiological limits and, second, that they do not all stop *in the same place*. And, if you are to succeed in stopping way short of where other people are stopping then you are going to have to do something much stronger than not collect some information you could have collected. You will have to *actively reject* information that others are trying to force on you. What I want to show is that, even within a single outfit (an Everest expedition, or a corporation or a society), there are always several mutually contradictory drawings of the line between information and noise. Information rejection, therefore, is the turning into noise of something that is already information to someone else.

(1)   "What you don't know can't harm you" (Anonymous)

(2)   "When I feel like reading a book, I write one" (Benjamin Disraeli)

(3)   "These preposterous theories of Professor Ohm..." (the scientific establishment's reaction to the first attempt to publish Ohm's Law).

---

45   This section is based on Thompson and Wildavsky (1986).

(4)   "If it was good enough for Moses then it's good enough for me" (fundamentalist song - "Gimme That Old Time Religion" - rejecting Darwin's theory of evolution).

These examples all involve information rejection, but I have selected them so that the *kind* of information rejected, and the *way* in which it is being rejected, are different in each case. If we ask ourselves, four times over, what the information rejection is being *used for* then we can uncover the distinct information rejecting styles that are being employed to support the different ways of organising (see Figure 4.1). In this way, *discourses* - arguing, as Sidney Smith put it, from different premises - become the very stuff of institutions: another point, I would claim, where cultural theory diverges from the mainstream.[46]

These four styles, I should stress, are *cultural* (or institutional) styles; they are reasonable responses to different transactional contexts: to different ways of being caught up in the process of social life. And, since each response is reasonable, this diagram is a typology of rationalities: a description of the different contexts that define what shall count as rational and what shall count as irrational. So this diagram is not rejecting the *theory of rational choice*; what it is saying is that, until we have this typology, we simply have not got a theory! To explain what I mean by "rationality-conferring contexts" let me quickly run through these four styles.

---

46   More water, however, has been flowing through the discourse channel in recent years, but mostly of a postmodernist kind that simply shows how what may appear to be hegemonic discourses are in fact being challenged by other equally valid discourses. In other words, there is no accompanying typology: no consideration as to how many different discourses there can be, or of how they self-organise through their mutual contentions and complementarities. For examples of cultural theory-based discourse analysis see Thompson, Rayner and Ney (1998) and Douglas, Thompson and Verweij (2003).

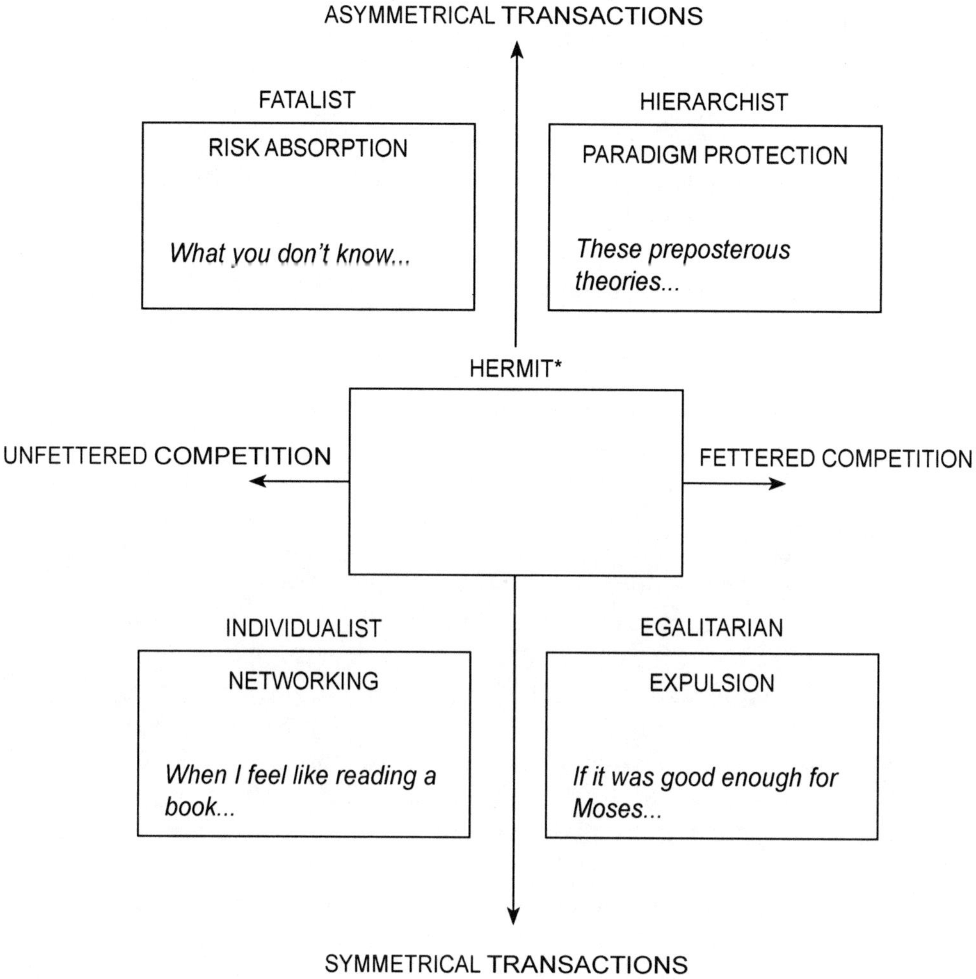
ASYMMETRICAL TRANSACTIONS
FATALIST
RISK ABSORPTION
What you don't know...
HIERARCHIST
PARADIGM PROTECTION
These preposterous theories...
HERMIT*
UNFETTERED COMPETITION
FETTERED COMPETITION
INDIVIDUALIST
NETWORKING
When I feel like reading a book...
EGALITARIAN
EXPULSION
If it was good enough for Moses...
SYMMETRICAL TRANSACTIONS

* The hermit's style of information rejection (which is the style the story-teller must adopt if he is to tell the plural rationality story) is characterised by an unwillingness to go along with any of these four styles, each of which he sees as being based on "erring ignorance".[47]

Figure 4.1: Information Rejecting Styles Mapped onto the Cultural Theory Diagram

47 The great Tibetan hermit, Milarepa, when pestered by a visiting (and clearly hierarchical) academic, burst into one of his famous songs: "Accustomed long to meditate upon the Whispered Chosen Truths, Knowledge of Erring Ignorance I've lost". (Evans-Wentz, 1954)

(1)   *Risk absorption* is practised by people for whom life is "like a lottery": the fatalistic acceptance of a world that does things to you without your being able to do anything to it. "Strategy" is really too strong a word to use for the way of coping that is the appropriate response in this sort of situation. *Individualised survival* is what it is all about; there is little point in kicking against the pricks, and the tough-minded acceptance of all the risks that you are powerless to deflect and that, like it or not, cascade down upon you, confers both realism and a certain measure of dignity.

(2)   *Networking.* Disraeli's problem is the danger of too much data, and he needs some deck-clearing principles - some methods for filtering out the data he can do without and for retaining the information (data organised for decision) which is absolutely vital. Time is in short supply and, alas, even he cannot be in more than one place at a time. He has a massive personal network that connects him to a lot of important people and he has, somehow or other, to shift the less important data onto those who are towards the periphery of his network so as to leave himself the time and space to listen to the most important information - to listen to those nearer the centre of his network. This social context, that of a very influential and very individualized person (an individualist), is quite familiar to those who have studied the implementation of information technology. Wynne and Otway (1982), for instance, have pointed out the reasonableness of the individualist's seemingly perverse preference for shifting the really vital discussions away from the formalized information-handling system and onto the informal "old boy net". We can characterize this strategy as *individualised manipulative.*

(3)   *Paradigm protection.* Professor Ohm has run foul of the scientific community (who had organised themselves around the study of static electricity), and what we see here is a closing of ranks by an establishment - by the upper tiers of a strongly hierarchical and power-wielding organizational form. Such organizational forms are not resistant to change itself (otherwise they would risk losing their power), but to those changes that threaten their hierarchical structure, causing information to

spill out of its proper channels, shortcutting correct procedures and, worst of all, questioning the paradigm on which the whole pyramid rests. Such information rejection is often diffused and depersonalized - the unseen discards from the agendas of committee meetings, and the sifting by shared (but unvoiced) assumptions that goes on in smoke-filled rooms.[48] When it is forced out into the open, it is usually swathed in an aura of altruistic self-sacrifice ("for the sake of the regiment", "in the national interest" and so on). The appropriate strategy here is *collectivised manipulative*.

(4)   *Expulsion.* In contrast to an establishment that uses information to monitor threats to its power and influence, there is another sort of grouping - one with no hierarchy - that takes a much more uncompromising and fundamentalist stand. A sect-like group, having no internal differentiation, has to concentrate all its defences at its boundary, protecting the soft vulnerable "us" from the nasty predatory "them" by a total rejection of threatening information. Since such egalitarian bounded groups do not negotiate and refuse to compromise with the wider society, they cannot manipulate anyone except their own members (who, of course, do not see this as manipulation, since it is what they voluntarily joined the group to do).[49] So the members of this sort of grouping sustain themselves with a *collectivised survival* strategy.

Now, with the typology of rallying points in place, and with it fleshed out both in terms of responses to leaderships and followerships and in terms of contending styles of information rejection, we have the essential framework for a theory of organising in which subversion is inevitable. Any theories that ignore subversion, or insist that it can (and should)

---

48   Nowadays the rooms are no longer smoke-filled, but the sifting still goes on!

49   Each way of organising, of course, generates its distinctive contradictions which, if unattended to, can easily undermine it. Marx's error was to think that this applied to only one "way of life" (capitalism) and not to that which he saw as replacing it (communism). A distinctively egalitarian contradiction (evident in several recent sieges and mass "suicides") arises when some of those who have voluntarily joined are prevented from leaving. For a list of the distinctive *tragedies* and *triumphs* that accompany the different ways of organising see the chart in Thompson (1992, pp199-202).

be got rid of, will be worse than useless. Good management, therefore, *must* be concerned with encouraging the constructive interplays of subversions and discouraging the destructive ones. That is the clumsy lesson we should learn from the Everest story.

CHAPTER 5

No Such Thing as an Organisation

Back in the 1980s (and as already recounted in Chapter 1) the United Nations Environment Programme UNEP) asked me to provide them with a systems framework that would enable them to get to grips with the environmental problems of the Himalaya (the Himalaya, along with the Amazon rain forest and the Sahel, being in what was then considered to be the first league of the world's environmental problems). As I tabulated the different rates at which different sorts of forest grow at different elevations, and confronted that complex (and extremely uncertain) information with the myriad (and often directly contradictory) interventions of United Nations organisations, bilateral aid agencies, national government departments, non-governmental organisations, multinational companies, small town businesses and, last but by no means least, the local subsistence farmers and the astonishingly varied farming systems that they operate, the full enormity of what I had taken on began to dawn on me.

"How to *manage* the Himalaya?", I finally realised, was the problem I had been handed. I therefore sought the help of a distinguished university's school of management. "Ah," said the head of the school, "that's not really a management problem". "Management, as we define it here," he continued, "is management *within* an organisation." The problem I had been handed, I learnt, had to do with "inter-organisational decision making" and that, much to his relief, was no concern of his.

As I waded, managerially unaided, into the Himalaya and their environmental problems I often found myself marvelling at the way *the organisation* so neatly separated these two kinds of decision making - intra-organisational and inter-organisational - and then dismissed the kind I was interested in from the field of management. Since beautifully clear-cut distinctions such as this are quite rare in the social sciences, I was intrigued when, some time later, I received an invitation to a conference (at a different university, I hasten to add) on "Aspects of Organisation".

Here, at last, was an opportunity for me - an anthropologist - to learn something about the theories of behaviour that underpin schools of management. My hopes were indeed realised, and in a splendidly destructive way!

The strong and, to my mind, very exciting message that emerged from that conference was this:

THERE ARE NO SUCH THINGS AS ORGANISATIONS;
THERE ARE ONLY WAYS OF ORGANISING AND WAYS OF
DISORGANISING.[50]

This is not to say that outfits such as the World Bank, Unilever, the UK Department for International Development, All Souls College and Greenpeace (to pick a fairly random bunch) do not exist. Of course, they *do*. Nor is it to say that such outfits are not organised. Of course, they *are*; otherwise they would not be able to come into existence and then go on existing and changing. No, what this is saying is that in none of these cases can the persistence of an outfit be accounted for in terms of just a single organising principle.

Though a chief executive, when quizzed about the nature of the beast he is endeavouring to control, may point to the neat pyramid-like diagram on his office wall, that is only part - his part - of the organisational story.[51] As he busies himself organising things that way, others, we may be sure, are busy organising things in other ways. "The word may come down from on high that pig-shit does not smell," say the lowerarchs to one another, "but we know that it does". Subversion, though it can be harnessed to constructive ends, can never be eliminated. Organisation is never singular. *An organisation*, therefore, is a contradiction in terms.

---

50   The conference - "Aspects of Organisation" - was held at Lancaster University and was organised by Gibson Burrell, Robert Cooper and Alan Whitaker. It was Robert Cooper who uttered the words that I found so exciting.

51   The vast French company Veolia (it operates around the world in the areas of water, energy, waste and transport) has banned "organigrams", which suggests that it is further down the inevitability of subversion road than many of its competitors.

What Now?

Once we accept this line of argument, the orthodox definition of what does and does not count as management collapses. This definition, we can now see, has been founded on the fallacy of misplaced concreteness: the assumption that there really *are* such things as organisations. Our attention, therefore, has to shift away from the non-existent organisations and onto the only things that do exist: the ways of organising and disorganising. The big questions now are:

1. What are these ways of organising and disorganising?

2. How many of them are there?

3. Why just these ones?

4. How do they interact? (That is, how do decisions get made *between* them?)

5. How do they co-exist? (That is, how come some of them don't, or even just one of them doesn't, disorganise the others out of existence?)

6. What leads a person to embrace one way rather than another?

7. Can people change from one way to another, and if so, how does this happen?

These are the questions that a theory of organisation that began from the premise *there is no such thing as an organisation* would have to answer.

My argument, of course, is that cultural theory is the only theory currently on offer that can answer all seven of these questions (though, as we will see, there are other theories and approaches that provide answers to some of them). Such an argument, like poor old Professor Ohm's, is going to ruffle a few disciplinary feathers because cultural theory comes from anthropology, not from departments of management and organisation. Nor can I smooth things over by pretending that cultural theory is simply feeding its humble two-penn'orth into the existing business school wisdom. After all, if there is no such thing as an organisation, which is what I am arguing, then all those learned establishments that insist on dealing only with management *within* an organisation must be dealing with nothing at all. The task, therefore, is not to improve the theory of organisation but to *create* it. All management teaching will have to concern itself with that which at present is excluded: "inter-organisational decision making".

Another important consequence of doing away with *the organisation* is that there is now no point along the scale dimension where organisations can be said to begin or end, which is rather a blow for institutionalists (new and old) who all insist that there is. Ways of organising and disorganising are at work at the level of the United Nations, at the level of the nation-state, at the level of the firm, at the level of the household and even, given that he or she is inherently relational, at the level of the individual. In other words, *cultural dynamics are independent of social scale.*

Ways of organising and disorganising, you could say, are like Mandelbrot's fractals,[52] or William Blake's "universe in a grain of sand". Each and every scale level is the microcosm of the one above it and macrocosm of the one below it. Each piece, like the DNA within the elephant, contains the whole. The ways of organising and disorganising, you could say, are to human life what the letters are to a stick of Blackpool rock. They go all the way through it; no matter where you happen to break into it, there they are!

The usual response to these two conclusions - that management science has no point of contact with its subject matter and that there is nothing fundamental about scale - is that I *can't* be serious. I am (though I do tend to agree with Oscar Wilde, had he actually said it, that some things are far too important to be taken seriously). One useful way of describing cultural theory is to say that it is a programme for the extermination of false dualisms. Its starting point, for instance, is the rejection of the individual/society dualism that has provided the unquestioned basis

---

52   For a non-technical explanation of what these are see Gleick (1987).

for most social theorising, and it now has two more in its sights: intra/ inter (as in management *within* an organisation) and micro/macro (as in micropolitics, macroeconomics and so on).

Five, And Just Five, Ways Of Organising

Let me quickly recapitulate cultural theory yet again, but in a slightly different way.

1. You can organise yourself into one of three *distinct patterns*: ego-focused groups (the individualist's pattern), bounded and ranked groups (the hierarchist's pattern) and bounded but unranked groups (the egalitarian's pattern). Alternatively, you can (if you take up the hermit's option) organise yourself against these three patterns. And, since patterns inevitably result in discards, you can find yourself on the outside of all four of these ways of organising. This last is the fatalist's externally prescribed predicament.

2. If you are to strengthen the pattern of which you are a part you will have to follow the *rationality* appropriate to that pattern. And if you are to justify your behaviour, to yourself and others, you will have to subscribe to the *myth of nature* that, by inculcating a particular set of convictions as to how the world is and people are, underpins that rationality.

3. These five ways of organising are all the ways there are (this is cultural theory's *impossibility theorem*) and each needs the others in its environment if it is to be viable (the *requisite variety condition*).

So the first three of my seven questions - "What are these ways of organising?", "How many of them are there?" and "Why just these ones?" - have now been answered. But is it really that easy? Can an impossibility theorem really appear, out of the blue like this, and wreak such havoc in the treasure-house of social thought?

A sticking point for many people, even after they have been exposed to the Schmutzer and Bandler proof, is the severe limitation of possible patterns that cultural theory insists on.[53] Clever proofs are all very well but why, many people still wonder, cannot there be other patterns? In the hope of persuading these doubters, let me now try to explain the impossibility theorem in the less rigorous, but more down-to-earth, language of pattern making and pattern breaking.

Possible Patterns

In what could be called a "perfect group", every member is connected to every other member and none of them is connected to anyone else. This means that, no matter which member you begin with, you will, when you have traced out all his or her connections, end up with exactly the same set of people: all the members of the group. With a network, this does not happen. Each person has his or her own network, with him or her at its centre. One person's network may, of course, overlap in some way with those of others, but you will never get two networks to coincide. In other words, one diagram will serve to depict the relationships of all the group members (a "collective representation", Durkheim would say) but there will have to be as many diagrams as there are people if the networks are to be full depicted.

In social science, this distinction has usually been interpreted as one of pattern versus non-pattern. Groups, clearly, are patterned but networks (because they spread all over the place, have no boundaries and are as numerous as the people who build them) have been seen as the result of when the patterns - the groups - break down. By contrast, cultural theory recognises that both groups *and* networks are patterns. We can establish the validity of this claim by showing that both groups and networks can break down. If networks were what you got when groups broke down then networks themselves would not be able to break down. If they *can* break down then the transition from groups to networks must involve not one but two stages: the dismantling of group patterns and the building up of network patterns.

---

53 Though cultural theorists find this a strange objection, given that their theory more than doubles the variety - hierarchies and markets, Gemeinschaft and Gesellschaft, etc - that social science has allowed up until now.

The easiest way of visualising the emergence of a group is to imagine a whole lot of unconnected points on a sheet of paper and to then let a sequence of relationships proliferate by linking point 1 to point 2 to point 3 and so on until eventually point n connects up with point 1 and you have a loop. Then all you have to do is move those unconnected points that are inside this loop to the outside and let the established relationships proliferate across this now empty space until every point in the loop is connected to every other point. You will then have a "perfect group" - one in which every possible internal connection is made and there are no connections from any member of that group to any point that is outside it ("strong connectedness" and "closure" in Schmutzer's and Bandler's terms). If your group is small in comparison to the total number of points you can go on repeating this sort of procedure until all the points have been gathered into isolated groups. The result will be a very definite pattern: a polka dot pattern (though the dots will be of different sizes, unless you have also specified the numerical value of n).

However, if you went for the maximum possible number of connections, by forming a loop that took in every single point and then connecting each of those points to all of the others, you would end up with no pattern at all. If everyone is related to everyone else then, in terms of their relationships, they are all the same. The same is true of the initial situation in which no one is related to anyone else. For there to be pattern, people must be related to some people and not to others. That is, pattern can only exist when some, but not all, possible connections have been made. By the same token, pattern will disappear if these connections become too few or too many. The next step, therefore, is to show that these same two patternless end-states apply to networks as well as to groups.

The easiest way of visualising the emergence of networks is to start with the same sheet of paper, covered in the same unconnected points, and to let relationships radiate out from one of those points to those that are immediately adjacent to it. Each of those points, in its turn, can be connected to all those points that are immediately adjacent to it, provided (and this is the crucial condition) they are closer to it than to any of the other points. And so on, until the proliferating relationships reach an edge of the sheet of paper. A fresh network can then be started by choosing one of the still unconnected points and repeating the same procedure, and so on. Eventually, all the points will be incorporated into distinct networks (each with its own central point). If you happen to have begun by choosing a point at the very centre of the sheet of paper you will have just one large star-like pattern. If you began with a point near an edge you will have a number of patterns of varying sizes butted up against one another, like frost on a window-pane. What you will not have, thanks to having followed the rule that each wave of proliferations must be to the most adjacent points, are any sequences of relationships that bend round on themselves to form a complete loop (which, of course, was the first stage for the formation of group patterns). In other words, networks do give you patterns, and those patterns are different in kind from those that you get with groups:

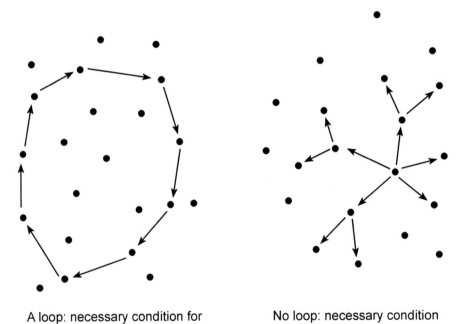

A loop: necessary condition for a *group*.

No loop: necessary condition for a *network*.

Figure 5.1: Two Kinds of Patterns

You could increase the number of connections, without destroying the patterns, if you allowed the networks to interpenetrate one another, and the number of connections would also increase the more networks there were to start with. But if you followed this principle to its logical conclusion, and allowed a network to proliferate from every point and to interpenetrate every other network, you would end up with exactly the same patternless end-state as you got with a group that included every point. Everyone would be connected to everyone else and they would all be identical in terms of relationships. In other words, networks, though they are different in kind from groups, start and finish with the same patternless end-states as do groups. This means that if relationships are gathered into groups they can only be gathered into networks by first breaking down those group patterns, and *vice-versa.*

Of course, just because both groups and networks are patterns, it does not follow that they (and their combination)[54] are the only patterns that can be formed with relationships. To prove that they are, you need Schmutzer and Bandler's mathematical argument. However, now that I have set out this more down-to-earth argument for the patterns, let me use it to explain another crucial feature of cultural theory: the *inherent relationality* of the individual.

Since the various patterns are always in competition for adherents, it is not enough that a person be part of a pattern. He or she must also support it, and you cannot support a pattern if you cannot *experience* it. "Distributed cognition" - shareable experience - is therefore a necessary condition for both pattern viability and individuality: cultural theory's *California condition* (from that joke about the number of Californians it takes to share the experience of changing a light-bulb). You cannot, for instance, be a hierarchist if you have no way of knowing that the relationships of you and your fellow hierarchists are hierarchical.[55]

---

54   A hierarchy, though usually depicted like a family tree, can be rearranged so that it radiates out from a central node (the topmost level) with the different "grades" then forming concentric circles; a pattern that is topologically identical to an ego-focused network, but formed of bounded groups and not "atomised" people.

55   Strictly speaking, you do not need to know that you are a hierarchist; only that you are *different from* those who are not hierarchists. Blackbirds, for instance, do not have to know that they are blackbirds; only that they are different from those birds (thrushes, starlings and so on) that are not blackbirds. Birds of a feather do not have to be ornithologists before they can flock together!

Group patterns present no problem here because, as we have already seen, you always get the same set of people no matter which group member you happen to choose as your starting point in tracing out the relationships. The fact that a single diagram works for every group member means that they can readily share their experience of the pattern of relationships they are caught up in. But the members of a network, having each their own diagram, cannot share their network experience in this sort of way (this, I suspect, is what has led so many social scientists to equate groups with pattern and networks with non-pattern). What *is* shareable about network involvement, however, is the common experience of *network centrality* (for those who have been forceful or lucky enough to forge relationships without serious restriction: symmetrical relationships that is) and *network peripherality* (for those who have found many of the relationships they might have forged "foreclosed" by their prior incorporation into the networks of others: asymmetrical relationships that is). In other words, the experience of network involvement is perceptible and shareable in terms of the *breaking of symmetry* that that involvement always entails (only if every individual's network took in everyone else, or if each one's network interpenetrated its neighbouring networks to the same degree, would there be no breaking of symmetry. In both these cases, as we have seen, everyone will be identical in terms of relationships and hence there will be no pattern).

What this means is that if you were to set up a social system in which individuals had to maximise their transactions but were forbidden to form themselves into groups you would end up, either with no pattern at all, or with two quite distinct experiential categories: network centralists (that is, individualists) and network peripheralists (that is, fatalists). These categories would, however, be altogether different from those that would be formed if you set up your social system on the contrary rule that transactions were to be maximised without the formation of ego-centred networks. The breaking of symmetry in that case would be between two experientially different kinds of groups: those (the egalitarians) whose members were maximising their transactions by keeping their groups apart from others and those (the hierarchists) who were maximising their transactions by arranging their groups (not themselves) into orderly and ranked relationships with other groups. Egalitarians, by keeping their groups unrelated to other groups (or to networks), are able to maximise their transactions by connecting every insider to every other insider: "perfect equality" in the cybernetic sense that there is both *closure* and strong *connectedness*. Hierarchists, by contrast, increase their transactional involvement by connecting themselves to other groups, but, as they do this, they inevitably impose some restrictions on the density of transactions within their group. Goods and services that are provided for them by others can no longer be provided by the group members and *vice versa*, otherwise there would be no way of differentiating between the groups, and it would no longer be possible to experience the inter-group involvement. Institutionalised "inequality", (in the cybernetic sense that there is *closure* and weak *connectedness*) therefore, is necessary if involvement in such a pattern of relationships is to remain shareable.[56]

Whilst each of these ways of transaction-maximizing gets going by organising itself against the other three,[57] they create, between them, the possibility for a fifth way of organizing: one in which, bizarre though it may seem, transactions are *minimized*. This, it turns out, gives us the hermit's solidarity (autonomy): a solidarity that, in contradistinction to the other four, is stabilized by the avoidance of all coercive social involvement. Since this way of organizing needs the maximizing ways so as to have something to organize itself against, we now have a plausible line of argument (though not of course, a proof) for the requisite variety condition.

In summary, cultural theory gives us five ways of organising, each of which defines itself against the others. The whole thing, therefore, is a self-organising system that cannot be simplified. If one way of organising is there they will all be there, and if one of them were to disappear they would all disappear. Of course, their relative strengths and patterns of alliance can vary (and I will come to these in a moment) and it is to these variations that we should look to understand why different social systems are different and why even the same system alters over time. In other words, there is nothing graven in stone that says "Once a hierarchist

---

56 It may be helpful here to refer back to chapter 3: the section headed "The Impossibility Theorem" (pp44-46).

57 Fatalists, to be precise, do not maximise their transactions. Their transactionally prescribed predicament is the unavoidable concomitant of all the transaction-maximising that is going on in the other three socially engaged forms of solidarity.

(or whatever), always a hierarchist (or whatever)". People can, and do, disengage themselves from one pattern and engage themselves in another. But of course, being dividuals, this disengagement is unlikely to be in every area of their lives. Swiss villagers, for instance (and as is explained in chapter 6) may switch from individualism to egalitarianism in their forest management when avalanches sweep through the sparse trees and threaten their homes, whilst remaining hierarchists in relation to their Alpine pastures and individualists in relation to their fields in the valley bottom.

The next step, as those readers who have now got the hang of this way of reasoning may have guessed, is to enquire whether this sort of movement is not just possible but vital. Could it be that organisation is like riding a bicycle: if you don't keep it rolling along you can't do it? If the answer is "Yes, it *is* like riding a bicycle" then yet another long-cherished dualism - stability versus change (static versus dynamic) - bites the dust.

No Change, No Stability

Bumping up the number of ways of organising from the conventional two of social science to the full complement - five - makes social change much more interesting. After all, if there are only markets and hierarchies then being dislodged from one means inevitably landing up in the other. Change in a two-destination world is inevitably *deterministic* and *predictable*. For instance, Margaret Thatcher's advisors predicted that a concerted attack on hierarchy - the trades unions, the professions, the nationalised industries, etc - would result in an "enterprise culture": a nation populated entirely with individualists.[58] And many pundits confidently predicted that, once the Soviet hierarchy had collapsed, the markets would spring up "like mushrooms".[59]

---

58 For an explanation of why this did not happen (or rather, why other unexpected things happened as well and in somewhat greater strength) see Thompson (1992).

59 For an explanation of why this did not happen (or, rather, why the mushrooms that did spring up were either oligarchs or mafias) see Intriligator, Wedel and Lee (2006).

But go beyond two and the whole picture changes. Even if you simplify things by leaving out the hermit, they are still complicated enough: 12 possible transitions (and including the hermit adds another 8):

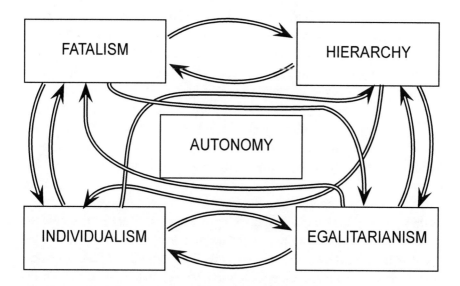

Figure 5.2: Possible transitions in a four or five destination world. (The eight transitions into and out of autonomy are omitted for the sake of clarity.)

If this is how things are then change is no longer deterministic, nor is it predictable. If you are tipped out of one way of organising then you will end up in one of the other three (four if you include the hermit) but you cannot say for certain which one. Then, when you are tipped out of that one, there are three possible destinations (four if you include the hermit) and so on, and on. If you build a little computer simulation - an *artificial life model* - of this sort of system (Thompson and Tayler, 1985) you will find, first, that it never settles down and, second, that it never exactly repeats itself. Nor, though they experience some tremendous ups and downs (accompanied, of course, by some tremendous learnings of certain lessons by the constituent social beings and unlearnings of others), do any of the contending solidarities ever go into permanent extinction. As long as "energy" is pumped in from the outside, this *disequilibrium system* goes on and on, lurching one possible way then another, and in this very process reaffirming the permanence of the destinations - the multiple attractors - without which those lurches would not be possible.

In other words, cultural theory tells us that social systems belong not to the well understood world of *Newtonian mechanics* but to *complexity*. The appropriate analogy is not the arrow (the one-way transition between A and B favoured by Durkheim, Weber, Marx, etc) nor is it even the pendulum (the oscillation between A and B favoured by Spencer, Leach, etc).[60] It is the flock of starlings, endlessly transforming itself (otherwise it could not stay airborne), continuously reaffirming the directions that make those transformations sufficiently varied (otherwise it could not stay a flock) yet never going anywhere.[61] Such a system is certainly ordered, and that orderliness is achieved only by continuous change, but you can predict nothing about that change beyond the prediction that things will not stay as they are. Order without predictability is what complex systems give us. That is why cultural theory focuses on the dynamics that generate the order and distances itself from the sorts of predictions to which "two-destination social science" aspires: another of cultural theory's major divergences from the mainstream. What, then, actually causes the transitions of dividuals from one way of organising to another: transitions that, we can now see, are vital to the continued existence of the whole?

Change, cultural theory argues, occurs because the five ways of organising, though socially viable, are not impervious to the real world. Just because people are insisting that the world is the way their myth of nature tells them it is, it does not follow that that is how the world really is. If it is then that is fine, but if it is not then they have got an uphill struggle ahead of them. *Surprise* - the outcome of the ever-widening discrepancy between

---

60   See Thompson, Ellis and Wildavsky (1990) Part II.

61   Some qualification is needed here; after all, flocks of starlings do not always stay in the same place! In chapter 3, in explaining the hermit's myth that endlessly cycles through the other four myths, the ball has to roll away into a new basin once the landscape has imploded. So we will need some theory to explain where that new basin comes from. Going round the cycle, we can hypothesise, results in the *emergence* of complexity that was not there before - a new "technological paradigm", for instance - and it is that that provides the new basin. This - the vital role of cycles in making linear change (evolution) possible - is a topic that requires a book all to itself (but see Tayler *circa* 1986).

the expected and the actual - is of central importance in dislodging people from their ways of organising. And it is these various mismatches between what a way of life promises and what it delivers that are all the time tipping people out of one way of organising and into one of the others. Of course, this hypothesis does require the world, at times and in places, to be each of these possible ways, otherwise we would all eventually end up surprised into the single true way. And it would help the surprises to keep on and on going if the world itself kept changing the way it was.

So the challenge we now face, and which I try to rise to in the next chapter, is to show that, strange though it may sound, this is indeed how the world is. The challenge, and the way in which I believe it can be risen to, can be put like this:

☐ No matter how lightly we tread on the Earth, we cannot avoid altering it. And, as it alters, so the way we tread on it - our ecological footprint, as it is sometimes called - is, in turn, altered. On and on. Natural scientists tend to look at this interaction of the human and the natural from the Earth's perspective, *The Earth as Transformed by Human Action* (Turner et al, 1990) being the classic text. Social scientists tend to look at the interaction from the socio-cultural end: *Living with Nature* (Fischer and Hajer, 1999), with its subtitle *Environmental Politics as Cultural Discourse*, is a recent example. But can we go further? Can we push each of these approaches (the natural scientist's and the social scientist's) to the point where they actually meet and give a single, unified theory of our relationship with nature?

"Yes we can", chorus two schools of thought: one sociological, the other ecological. The first, which has its roots in social anthropology, is, of course, the theory of socio-cultural viability that goes by the less cumbersome name, cultural theory. The second, which we have already encountered in connection with the ball-and-landscape myths of nature, has emerged from natural resource ecology, where those whose interest is in grasslands, fisheries, forests and so on encounter the institutions that are doing the exploiting and the managing, not as organised arrangements of people and their various convictions as to how the world is, but as patterned interventions in the ecosystems they are studying.

CHAPTER 6

Man and Nature as a Single but Complex System[62]

The classic assumption, in both ecology and social science, is that there is a one-way transition from state A to state B. In ecology, the process of succession (Clements, 1916; Odum, 1969) ensures that an initially unstructured state of affairs (one huge niche filled with anarchic, opportunistic and competitive organisms - the r-strategists, as they are called) is steadily transformed into a climax community: a structured and stratified arrangement of diversified niches, with clearly defined interrelationships between the species - the k-strategists, as they are called - that occupy them. In social science, this predictable, linear and equilibrium-seeking model of change is paralleled by a number of grand theories (we will be looking at these in more detail in the next but one chapter) in which some inexorable logic moves us all from mechanical to organic solidarity (Durkheim, 1893); from community to society (Gemeinschaft to Gesellschaft, Tönnies, 1887); from traditional to modern (Weber, 1922); from status to contract (Maine, 1861); from capitalism to communism (Marx, 1859); or, as modern theorists of institutions put it, from markets to hierarchies (Lindblom, 1977; Williamson, 1975). Different masters may define their As and their Bs differently, but all subscribe to a two-fold scheme and to some driving force (such as rationalization, internal contradiction, or spiralling transaction costs) that carries the totality from A to B.[63]

These transitions, whether ecological or socio-cultural, are all in the direction of more orderliness, more differentiation, more connectedness, and more consistency and, once they have gone as far as they can go in that direction, that is that. In other words, these models of change end up making change impossible. Of course, something on the outside

---

62 This chapter is based, in large part, on Thompson (2002) which, in turn, is largely based on Price and Thompson (1997).

63 In the cases of Lindblom and Williamson, the driving forces can go into reverse and take things from B to A as well (for example, transaction costs, in some circumstances, can spiral down).

may intervene and mess things up, thereby setting the whole thing in motion once more but, left to themselves, these models get ecosystems and socio-cultural systems from A to B and then stop. Change, these models tell us, is a temporary phenomenon.

These models are beginning to be seen as less than satisfactory. They explain change by getting rid of it, and they are increasingly incapable of making sense of what is actually going on. Not surprisingly, in view of these shortcomings, they have now been challenged by models that are indeterministic (i.e. more than two-fold) and make change a permanent and essential feature of existence: the fourfold institutional scheme proposed by cultural theory and the fourfold *ecocycle* advanced by Holling (1986). If social and ecological systems are as these models say they are, their interaction will inevitably result in complex and non-linear dynamics, giving an unpredictable, always out of equilibrium, and never-ending sequence of transitions between multiple states. And none of these will ever be the end of the road.

In the classic social science formulation, two kinds of solidarity interact. *Markets* are the competing players, all merrily bidding and bargaining with one another; *hierarchies* are the benign authorities who ensure that the various conditions for the playing of this trading game (a level playing field, for instance) are in place. Cultural theory, as we have seen, does not reject this foundational distinction. Rather, it argues that there is more to life than just markets and hierarchies and that you will lay yourself open to all sorts of unwelcome surprises - the Brent Spar fiasco, for instance, and the non-appearances of Margaret Thatcher's enterprise culture and Russia's market mushrooms - if you go on assuming that hierarchies and markets explain it all.

- The analysis (set out, in some detail, below) of how things are actually done in Himalayan and Alpine villages makes clear that, if these farmers were relying on just markets and hierarchies, neither they nor their supporting environments would be the way they are.

- In a parallel argument, but at a higher scale level, the ills of the American city have been convincingly blamed on the public-private partnerships (PPPs, as they are now commonly called) that are seen as the solution (Brion 1992). Hierarchies and markets, in coming together in this cosy and unseemly way (Brion identifies the actual club in one city - Philadelphia - where these dodgy deals have been done), have excluded community (i.e. the egalitarian solidarity) and forced the citizenry into a state of "atomized, alienated subordination and systematic exploitation" (i.e. fatalism).

- And at the highest scale level of all - the global - the three active solidarities (markets, hierarchies and egalitarianism) together with the markedly different problem definitions and solution definitions that each of them generates, are clearly discernible in the climate change debate. Indeed (harking back to chapter 4 and my point about discourses being the very stuff of institutions) they are what make that debate possible, each voice all the time defining itself in contradistinction to the other two. Hierarchists pin the blame on population. Individualists (the supporters of the market-based solidarity, which cultural theorists call individualism) see it as stemming from people being able to treat the environment as a free good. Egalitarians insist that it is profligacy (excessive consumption, especially in the richest nations of the world) that is the root of it all.[64] Their solutions - essentially, reduce population (hierarchy), get the prices right (individualism) and frugality (egalitarianism) - are so divergent that each constitutes part of the other two's problems. Frugality, it turns out, requires the abdication of capitalism: the driving force of the individualist's solution. The population diagnosis, as far as the egalitarians are concerned, blames the victim, (the South, which is where all the population growth is), and lets the guilty party, the North, off the hook. And the sorts of market interventions that both the hierarchists and the egalitarians, in their different ways, are intent on will, the individualists insist, get the prices even more wrong than they are at present!

---

64   This, to be precise, is how the definitions were back in the early 1990s (see Chapter 4, Volume 1 of Rayner and Malone 1998, where the self-organisation of these three voices is set out by means of a painstaking discourse analysis). For a discourse analysis of the same debate a decade later see Douglas, Thompson and Verweij (2003).

What all this means is that human interactions with the environment, wherever they may be on the local-to-global scale, cannot be effectively analysed using theoretical frameworks that allow just one or two positions. Such frameworks are *insufficiently variegated*.

This is the main practical message from cultural theory, and it is a highly discomforting message for policy makers generally and, in particular, for those who build the computer-based models that underlie most policy making within the broad area that is now labelled "sustainable development".[65] In most of these models, the representation of the micro-level, the household (in energy modelling) and the farmer (in land-use modelling), is singular: an economically rational utility maximizer. Such a representation recognizes just one voice (that of individualist solidarity) and silences the other two.

More recently, modellers have progressed to the classic formulation and recognized two of the voices. The International Geosphere Biosphere Programme - Land-Use and Land-Cover Change (IGBP-LUCC) project, for instance, notes that land-use and land-cover change is taking place increasingly under the influence of the market, and that this justifies a model based on economic theory: a decentralized set-up in which all agents individually solve their inter-temporal maximization problems, consumers maximizing utility, firms maximizing profits and so on. If the markets are competitive, so the argument runs, these agents can take prices as given, but in those instances where markets are not competitive, the optimization has to be done by government or some other higher level authority. But the third voice (that of egalitarian solidarity) is still excluded, leaving the policies that such models underpin wide open to the

---

65 Sustainable development, cultural theorists would point out, only makes sense if you are equipped with the hierarchist's myth of nature: Nature Perverse/Tolerant (see Figure 2.1). Development within the "pocket of stability" is sustainable, but if it lies outside this pocket ("beyond the limits", as it is so often said) it is unsustainable. But in the individualist's myth (Nature Benign) *all* development is sustainable, and in the egalitarian's myth (Nature Ephemeral) *no* development is sustainable!

Policy debates that are framed in terms of sustainable development, therefore, impose a *hegemonic discourse*, with non-hierarchical voices being muted to the point where there is very little in the way of either access or responsiveness (see Figure 1.5): *closed hegemony*, in other words, when what is needed is the opposite: *clumsy institution*.

sorts of nasty surprises that have overtaken Shell and the government in Britain, the public-private urban regeneration partnerships in the United States, the state and its long-suffering citizens in Russia, and so on.

Two-voice modelling, though an improvement, is still insufficiently variegated. Like one-voice modelling, it is still wedded to optimization and managerial control, when what is needed is constructive and argumentative engagement (as happened with Arsenal and its new stadium) between all the voices: the democratization, in other words, of decision processes that have been depoliticized and treated as merely technical. This is a topic that, since the debacles over mad cow disease (bovine spongiform encephalopathy) and genetically modified crops in Britain, the dismantling of the Millau MacDonald's by the French sheep farmer José Bové, the Battles of Seattle and Prague (vehement demonstrations against the World Trade Organization), and a host of similar events around the world, is increasingly on national and international agendas. But, to actually do that democratizing, we have to avoid silencing any of the voices, and that is something that current approaches, being insufficiently variegated, cannot do.

To help clarify what sort of differences a sufficiently variegated framework makes, and to gain a more reflexive understanding of what is going on in our own social systems and environments, we can take a close look at the surprisingly complex lives of the seemingly simple folk who live in the Himalaya and the Alps.[66] These people, cultural theorists would point out, know something that the single problem-single solution merchants who tend to dominate policy-making in advanced industrialized societies have managed to forget.

---

66   Reflexivity means the self-conscious examination of the assumptions that underlie any analytical approach: something that is easily said but not easily done. Indeed, since there is no "cosmic exile" - no "station in the clouds" from which we can gain the clear and undistorted view that full reflexivity demands - it cannot be done. Hence the whole round-the-corner approach by way of cultural theory, clumsiness, analyses in terms of access and responsiveness and so on.

Solidarities in Action

Himalayan villagers parcel out their transactions with their physical environment to four distinct solidarities, each of which is characterized by a distinct management style. Agricultural land, for instance, is privately owned whilst grazing land and forests are communally owned. But grazing land and forests do not suffer the "tragedy of the commons"[67] because transactions in their products are under the control of a commons-managing institution. Villagers appoint forest guardians, erect a social fence (a declared boundary, not a physical construction) and institute a system of fines for those who allow their animals into the forest when access is forbidden, or take structural timber without first obtaining permission. If the offender is also a forest guardian, the fine is doubled; if children break the rules, their parents have to pay up.

Informal though they may seem and lacking any official legal status, these arrangements work well in the face-to-face setting of a village, with its physical resources. Drawing on their home-made conceptions of the natural processes that are at work (their *ethnoecology*), the forest guardians regulate the use of these common property resources by assessing their state of health, year by year or season by season. In other words these transactions are regulated within a framework that assumes, first, that you can take only so much from the commons and, second, that you can assess where the line between so much and too much should be drawn. The social construction inherent to this transactional realm is that nature is bountiful within knowable limits. This, to make a link back to the cultural theory argument set out in chapter 2 (and forward to the ecological theory I am about to set out) is the myth of Nature Perverse/ Tolerant (see Figure 2.1).

---

67   The Tragedy of the Commons (Hardin 1972) is when every individual can see that the pasture is being destroyed by overgrazing, yet no single individual is prepared to reduce the number of cows he is putting onto the common. The tragedy is usually portrayed as inevitable, human nature being what it is asserted to be (i.e. self-seeking: the individualist myth of nature), in which case the only solution (apart from heavy-handed policing) is to privatize the commons (or "clarify property rights", as economists say). Yet anthropologists (and others) can point to countless common property resources around the world - fisheries, grazing lands, forests and so on - that do *not* suffer the tragedy of the commons.

With agricultural land, however, decisions are entirely in the hands of individual owners, and fields (unlike communally owned resources) can quite easily end up belonging to the moneylenders. In recent years, when forests and grazing lands have suffered degradation (for a variety of reasons, not the tragedy of the commons),[68] villagers have responded by shifting some of their transactions from one realm to the other. For instance, they have allowed trees to grow on the banks between their terraced fields (thereby reducing the pressure on the village forest) and they have switched to stall-feeding their animals (thereby making more efficient use of the forest and grazing land and receiving copious amounts of manure which they can then carry to their fields[69]). In other words, transactions are parcelled out to the management styles that seem appropriate and, if circumstances change, some of those transactions can be switched from one style to another.

Since they are subsistence farmers, whose aim is to remain viable over generations (rather than to make a killing in any one year) their transactions within their local environment can be characterized as low risk □ low reward. However, during those times of the year when there is little farm work to be done, many villagers engage in trading expeditions, or in migrant labour in India.[70] Trading expeditions are family based, family financed and highly speculative: high risk □ high reward. So a farmer's individualized transactions, when added together over a full

---

68 In the 1950s, following the overthrow of the Rana regime, Nepal's forests were nationalised and brought under the control of the state forestry service. This destroyed the village-level commons-managing institutions and then did not work itself (there was a lack of trust among the villagers and all sorts of obstacles to effective control by the state forestry service). A half century later, these shortcomings have been addressed: control has been handed back to the village-level (forest user groups), the forestry service has taken on a more advisory role, and community forests are flourishing.

69 Or use to generate biogas, which, as well as supplying the fuel for the household's cooking needs, leaves a residue that is an even better fertiliser than the original manure.

70 In recent years this strategy has expanded to working in the Gulf States, Malaysia, Korea and, of course Europe and the United States. Indeed, something like one in ten Nepalis are now engaged in this "remittance economy". Of course, they can no longer come back for each planting and harvesting season, and the result has been a marked detensification of their farming systems: fewer methane-emitting domestic animals and more carbon-sequestering trees.

year, constitute a nicely spread risk portfolio. The attitude here (and particularly at the high risk end of the portfolio) is that "Fortune favours the brave", "Who dares, wins", "There's plenty more fish in the sea". Opportunities, in other words, are there for the taking. The idea of nature here is optimistic, expansive and non-punitive: Nature Benign. (See Figure 2.1.)

Social scientists in general, and institutional economists in particular, would see these two realms as corresponding to their classic distinction between hierarchies and markets and would have no difficulty in explaining the processes by which some transactions are switched this way or that (though they would be surprised to find that the hierarchy was a village-level commons-managing institution, not the state). But (and this of course is the essence of the cultural theory argument) hierarchies and markets do not exhaust the transactional repertoire of the Himalayan villager. Some collectivized transactions do not involve formal status distinctions (such as those between forest guardians and ordinary villagers) and some individualized transactions are marked by the absence of bidding and bargaining (an essential characteristic of the markets that are generated by the individualist solidarity). The plurality, in other words, is four-fold, not two-fold.[71]

In many parts of the Himalaya (especially the Indian Himalaya), village autonomy is always under threat, because powerful outside actors are also laying claim to the forest resources that are so vital to Himalayan farming systems. One very effective response to this external threat has been the Chipko Movement. This is a grassroots and highly egalitarian social movement, in which women (who are largely responsible both for fodder gathering and fuelwood collection) predominate. *Chipko* means to stick, and the Gandhian strategy is to physically hug the trees, thereby preventing them from being appropriated. Those villagers of a slightly less non-violent disposition actually chase the logging contractors (and the government forestry officers who have been corrupted by the contractors) out of the forest with their *kukris* (long curved knives). In the Narmada

---

71   I am over-simplifying here, of course, by leaving out the autonomous solidarity. For an explanation of the hermit's not inconsiderable role in Himalayan life see Thompson (1982).

Valley, farther to the south (where a vast development project is under way), they have now done the same to the representatives of the World Bank: a South Asian counterpart to the Brent Spar surprise. (Indeed, the World Bank pulled out in 1993 but the project is still being promoted by Indian State Government and market borrowings.)

So far as these threatening external transactions are concerned, it is certainly not a case of "plenty more fish in the sea", nor is there even a safe limit within which the commercial extraction of timber would be sustainable. All external predation is seen as catastrophic in its consequences. Hence the spectacularly uncompromising collectivist response of the tree huggers, whose idea of nature is one in which any perturbation of the present low-key regime is likely to result in irreversible and dramatic collapse: Nature Ephemeral. (See Figure 2.1.)

Finally, in every village, we may be sure, there will always be some people who sneak wood from the forest when no one is looking, who can never quite get together the capital, the contacts and the oomph to go off on trading expeditions, and who manage somehow not to be around when it's all hands to the tree hugging. These are the fatalists: people whose transactions are somehow dictated by the organisational efforts of those who are not themselves fatalists. Theirs is a life in which the world is always doing things to them (sometimes pleasant, sometimes unpleasant) and in which nothing that they do seems to make much difference. "Why bother?" is the not unreasonable response of the fatalist. If that is how the world is, then learning is not possible and even if it were, there would be no way of benefitting from it. The idea of nature here is one in which things operate without rhyme or reason: a flatland in which everywhere is the same as everywhere else: Nature Capricious. (See Figure 2.1.)

From Simple to Complex

Completing the typology with these two solidarities (egalitarianism and fatalism) produces some important differences. For instance, once we understand the egalitarian solidarity, we can avoid the sorts of surprises that have been visited upon the Brent Spar and the Narmada River Project. And we can see that only if all the transactions are in the fatalistic realm (the one realm where learning is not possible) would the prevalent assumption (evident, for instance, in the hierarchist's diagnosis of the climate change problem) that there is a direct relationship between population increase and environmental degradation hold true.[72] But there is much more to it than this.

Change, in the conventional theory, is deterministic. If there are only two possible destinations then leaving one means ending up in the other, and *vice versa*. But if, as cultural theory insists, there are four (or, more properly, five) possible destinations the whole dynamical system becomes indeterministic: leave A and you can end up in B or C or D. And then, when you are dislodged from whichever of those you have landed up in, there are again three possible destinations; on and on. Where conventional theory has assumed that social systems are simple (linear, deterministic, insensitive to initial conditions, equilibrium-seeking and predictable), cultural theory treats them as complex (non-linear, indeterministic, sensitive to initial conditions, far from equilibrium, and unpredictable). Simple systems are manageable in the sense that, once we understand enough about them, we can define some desirable state of affairs - sustainable development is the current favourite - and then steer the totality towards it. But this, as my next example makes clear, is not possible if the system is complex.

A Swiss Example

Moving from the Himalaya to the Alps, we find much the same four-fold allocation of transactions, with agricultural land being privately owned and grazing land (and sometimes the forests) being communally owned. But the Swiss forests, unlike those of the Himalayan villagers, are physically sandwiched between the high pastures (communally owned) and the valley floor (privately owned fields, houses and hotels). Over the centuries that the Davos valley has been settled, to take a specific locality, both the fields and the grazing land have expanded at the expense of the forest. But the trees on the steeper intervening slopes have stayed in place, acting both as a source of timber and as a barrier against avalanches. However, it is difficult to achieve both these functions

---

72   The same assumption underlies the much-relied on IPAT equation: that Impact
      (i.e. environmental degradation) is some multiplication of Population, Affluence
      and Technology (see Ehrlich and Holdren 1974).

simultaneously, and the Davosers have often set in train changes in the forest's age structure which, decades later, have resulted in exceptional avalanches reaching the valley floor and threatening the destruction of the entire community.

Every time this unpleasant surprise has befallen them, the Davosers have responded by switching their forest management onto the "all in the same boat" egalitarian style. Later, it has sometimes shifted to the hierarchist style, often to the individualist style (with farmers owning long thin strips of forest running all the way from valley floor to alpine pasture), and sometimes to the fatalist style (as happened, for instance, when the avalanche danger was clearly perceived yet extraction continued in response to the demands of various mining booms and, in more recent years, the demand for ski-runs).

Surely, you might think, they would have got it right by now, but to think that is to assume that there is one right way. However, there is no way of ever getting it right, because managing one way inevitably changes the forest, eventually to the point where that way of managing is no longer appropriate. This would happen even if there were no exogenous changes (like the mining and tourist booms) which, of course, there always are (even in seemingly remote places like the Himalaya). Viability can only be achieved, therefore, by covering all the bases: by the villagers ensuring that they have the full four-fold repertoire of management styles, and by their being prepared to try a different one whenever the one they are relying on shows signs of no longer being appropriate. The Davosers, like their Himalayan counterparts, have now been in their valley for more than 700 years, without destroying either themselves or their valley in the process. This achievement would not have been possible if they had opted for just one management style, or even for the two that the prevalent orthodoxy allows!

Multi-vocality

Himalayan and Alpine villages, with their transactions parcelled out in these four very different ways, are impressively multi-vocal. More than that, as is evident from the examples of stall feeding and trees on private land (in the Himalaya) and of alternative forest management styles (in the Alps), they have the ability to switch transactions from one way to another whenever it seems likely that this might be more appropriate. Since the behaviour of the villagers is continually altering the resource base on which they depend, their villages would not be viable if they did not have this in-built (messy, noisy and argumentative) mechanism. What we have here, therefore, are high scores on both *access* and *responsiveness*, together with the high *deliberative quality* that that combination gives rise to. In other words (referring back to Figure 1.5) we are in the same province on the three-dimensional "landscape" as was the "policy sub-system" that came up with Arsenal's new stadium: *clumsy institution*.

To understand just how remarkable clumsy institutions are, imagine for a moment that you are some God-like experimenter, able to reach out and change this or that variable in a Himalayan village's environment, or to move it bodily east or west, north or south, across the convoluted landscape. As you bring in the logging contractors, or take it 100km eastwards or 1000m higher, the village will shift its transactions this way or that between its four options until it has adapted itself to its changed circumstances. In other words, it will maintain its viability thanks to the very practical learning system that is part and parcel of its four-fold plurality. If the village did not have this plurality, and was an elegant and unclumsy institution, like many national forestry services, including Britain's Forestry Commission (Tomkins, 1989) and the United States Forest Service (Hirt, 1994), it would not be able to do this. Something along these imaginary lines, it turns out, is what has actually happened, and continues to do so.

As we go from one Himalayan village to another, the relative strengths of the four ways of organizing vary. Egalitarianism, for instance, is strongest in those parts of the Himalaya that are most prone to commercial logging. As one moves eastwards, from India (with its powerful centre and its colonial heritage of Reserved Forests) into Nepal and Bhutan, so the Chipko Movement and its counterparts become less of a force to be reckoned with. If the inequitable external threat is absent then so too, it appears, is the communitarian response to it (as was the case with Arsenal Football Club and the rapid emergence of the Highbury Community Association, once the threat became evident). However, the most dramatic of these variations is north-south: between the strongly individualized Buddhist villages and the strongly collectivized Hindu villages a day or two's walk downstream. These are Fürer-Haimendorf's (1975) adventurous traders and cautious cultivators, respectively: apt characterizations which readily map onto two of the five social beings (individualists and hierarchists, respectively) in the cultural theory typology.

The term "social being" (to reiterate a crucial but not easily grasped argument) denotes the behaviour to which a dividual must conform, and the convictions he or she must espouse, in order to sustain the form of social solidarity to which he or she belongs. The terms hierarchist, individualist, egalitarian and so on thus denote available roles (or management strategies) that people step into, or out of, as their daily lives, or the changing seasons, take them from one transactional realm to another (see Box 6A: A Swiss Villager's Day). Similar boxes could be used to summarise our Buddhist and Hindu villagers' days and, as with our Swiss villager, we would see that all the roles are present. But the relative strengths of those roles - the proportion of transactions parcelled out to each - would vary, with more transactions being in the individualist quadrant in the Buddhist village and more in the hierarchical quadrant in the Hindu village.

During the growing season a villager may on one day milk his cows, cut hay, thin saplings, maintain an avalanche control structure and wash dishes in a restaurant. The cows, though privately owned, are grazed on pasture owned by a specific set of long-established families. The hay is on his own private field; the saplings are part of a forest owned by another set of families; the avalanche control structure is on private land but maintained by agreement by the village; and the restaurant is owned by a multinational hotel chain.

This framework is fairly stable from season to season but the villager has a very different pattern of activity in the winter when the cows live in his private byre and much of the land is snow-covered and barely used unless the valley includes a ski resort. If it does, then he has opportunities for work without leaving the valley. If not then he may leave to work elsewhere, thereby reducing the use of scarce resources at home. Thus in winter the human ecosystem centred on the valley is concurrently simpler and wider.

So our Swiss villager has a portfolio of transactions and management styles that fluctuates with the seasons and also with the longer-term dynamics (such as those that, in altering the age-structure of the forests, can eventually shift a whole category of transactions from one style to another).

- Like his Himalayan counterpart, he owns his hayfields and cows. These are private property; he can buy or sell them acting as an individualist, subscribing to the myth of Nature Benign.

- Coming from an old-established family, he is a member of a forest cooperative (Waldgenossenschaft) that gives him specific rights to cut trees and imposes a duty to maintain the forest. He is also a member of a pasture cooperative (Alpgenossenschaft) which annually decides the grazing season and the number of animals he may graze and requires him to contribute to the cowherd's upkeep. These are small-scale hierarchical institutions which have developed over the generations (in between the periods when the forests are privatized and their associated transactions transferred to the more exploitative individualist management style) in response to the limitations as well as the opportunities imposed by the natural environment: Nature Perverse/Tolerant.

- As a voting member of the commune, he also has a duty to maintain resources that contribute to its survival such as the avalanche control structures that protect houses, fields and roads from damage. This tends to be an egalitarian involvement which recognizes that, when it comes to these sorts of hazards, all the members of the community are in the same boat and that each should contribute his equal share: Nature Ephemeral.

- Lastly, as a dishwasher in a multinationally owned restaurant, he is effectively a replaceable fatalist. His involvement is necessary if the enterprise is to continue but he has no interest in its future nor it in his and he can be paid off at any time (he will almost certainly lose his job at the end of the summer season).

Box 6A: A Swiss villager's day

Fürer-Haimendorf (1975), having characterised the Hindu and Buddhist villages in terms of this strategic distinction, then shows how the small agricultural surpluses of the cautious cultivators become the payloads of the adventurous trader's yaks as they set off on their journey into Tibet, and how the salt they bring back eventually finds its way to the cautious cultivators who cannot themselves produce this vital commodity. The distinctive strategy of each thus makes viable the other's, and we begin to see how it is that each village, in adjusting to its circumstances (which include the other villages), creates and takes its place in a social and cultural ecosystem, in which the marked divergence of the parts sustains the whole. Nor is this a fanciful analogy. As I will show below, the adventurous trader's strategy matches that of the omnivorous and opportunistic r-selected species; the cautious cultivator's strategy matches that of the specialized and niche-dependent K-selected species. The fatalists do for social systems what compost does for natural systems (provides a generalized resource for renewal). Whilst the egalitarians, through their small-scale communal fervour, are creating enclaves of low-level energy (what Marx called primitive capital) in places where neither the r-selected nor the K-selected species can make any impression (Holling, 1986; Thompson *et al.*, 1990; Holling *et al.*, 1993).

So the ambitious hypothesis that is being sketched here is very different from the way people usually think about the interactions of social and natural systems. There is, on this view, no way of ever getting it right: of bringing the social into long-term harmony with the natural (which, of course, is the whole idea behind sustainable development). Instead, each is a four-fold and plurally responsive system, and their time-lagged interactions ensure that there can be no steady-state outcome. The whole system is in a perpetual unsteady state: changes at each level (the social and the natural) adapting to the other and changing it in the process, thereby setting in motion another set of changes. On and on. Nor are these changes predictable, as they would be if each level had only two possible states: hierarchies and markets, for instance, or, as is discussed below, their ecological analogues. Order without predictability (as opposed to transition from A to B, or oscillation between A and B, that the two-fold hypotheses give us) is the crucial idea behind this Himalayan story.

Theories of change that make change permanent

Change, cultural theory argues, occurs because the four[73] forms of social solidarity are not impervious to the real world. As I have already stated, just because people insist that the world is as their myth of nature tells them it is, it does not follow that the world really is so. If it is, that is fine, but if it is not, they have an uphill struggle. Surprise (the outcome of the ever widening discrepancy between the expected and the actual) is thus of central importance in dislodging people (and their transactions) from their form of social solidarity. And it is these various mismatches between what a way of life promises and what it delivers that continually tip people (and transactions) out of one form of social solidarity and into another. For that to happen and go on happening (and as I have already mentioned in the concluding section of the previous chapter), the world, at times and in places, will have to be each of these possible ways (otherwise we would all end up surprised into the one true way, after which no more change!). Moreover, change would fizzle out if surprises stopped coming, and this makes the proviso "at times" crucial. Not only has the world to be each of these possible ways as we go from place to place, it also has to be changing over time in each of these places. Cultural theory cannot fill in this part of the hypothesis, so we must turn to ecology.

Some ecologists (for instance, Holling 1986 and Holling et al 1993) have taken a similar tack to cultural theory and have elaborated the notion of requisite variety (which, coming from cybernetics, is as valid for ecosystems as it is for socio-cultural systems) into a powerful critique of the conventional idea that the *climax community* - the ecosystem in which each specialized species has its stable and ordered niche - is the end of the organisational road. This critique, of course, exactly parallels cultural theory's dissatisfaction with the conventional hierarchies-and-markets account of things, in that it argues that there must be four rather than just two destinations. Holling's critique is that the climax community eventually complexifies itself to the point where it undermines its own stability: an inevitable collapse, which has been proved mathematically by May (1982). This does not mean that an entire climax community

---

73   More properly five, of course but, as I have already explained, I am simplifying a
     little.

(the Amazon rain forest, for instance) will suddenly disappear, but it does require any climax community to be patchy: always to include some localized areas in collapse as, for instance, happens when a mature tree crashes to the ground.

At this catastrophic moment, all the energy that is tied up in all the niches and interdependencies of the climax community is released. Holling, well aware of the parallel with Schumpeter's (1950) theory of economic maturity, collapse and renewal, refers to the transition from the climax community to compost, as *creative destruction*. Nor, he argues, is this the end of the road. With the whole place suddenly awash with capital (loose energy), the challenge is to fix it before it all disappears, by soil leaching, for instance. This, of course, is where the unspecialized and cooperative fence builders (micro-organisms mostly) come into their own, gathering up the loose energy into small bundles that, as yet, have no connections with one another. But even this is not the end of the road, because the stage is now set for the appearance of yet different ecological players. These are the unspecialized but opportunistic, fast breeding and highly competitive r-selected species. These generalized exploiters (weeds, rodents and so on) are able to harness all the energy gradients that are now in place between all these unconnected bundles of energy. But these r-selected species, as they exploit and colonize this environment, inevitably begin to push it into a rather more patterned and interconnected state, thereby making it less conducive to their way of doing things and more suited to the sort of energy-conserving strategies that characterize the K-selected species: those specialized, slower breeding and often symbiotic plants and creatures, which are the vanguard of the complex and increasingly ordered whole that constitutes the climax community.

In other words, once you bump up the number of ecological strategies from two to four, there is no end to the road. Indeed, there is a never ending sequence, switching this way and that among the twelve kinds of transition that this fourfold scheme makes possible, that exactly parallels (in terms of dynamics, not substance) the social transitions of cultural theory.[74] Holling goes on to argue that, while all twelve of these transitions

---

74 I should stress that (unlike, say, sociobiology) there is no reductionism here. Phenomena at the socio-cultural level are not being explained in terms of what is going on at the biological level.

do happen, there is a tendency for some to predominate at certain stages, thereby creating a fairly regular sequence of transitions: from specialized interdependence (the climax community) to unstructured fragmentation (compost) to unspecialized cooperation (energy fixing) to unspecialized competition (the pioneer community) to specialized interdependence (the climax community, again) and so on. He calls this sequence an ecocycle, and its description (which can be supplemented with descriptions of all the other cycles that are possible but, Holling believes, less pronounced) helps us to see the gulf (some might use the expression paradigm shift) that separates this model of change from the conventional one:

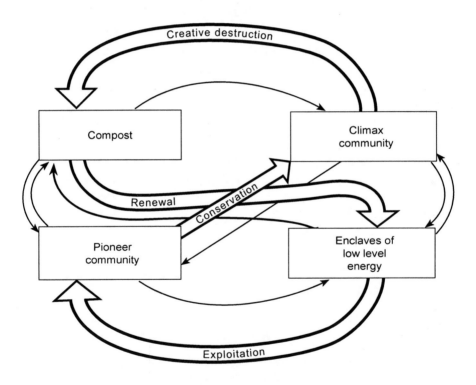

Figure 6.1: The complex critique of the conventional assumptions about natural systems (redrawn from Holling, 1986 to be homologous with Figure 5.2)

Is there, then, a socio-cultural equivalent of Holling's ecocycle? Yes, there is, and it can be most easily set out by reference to the theory of surprise: the theory that provides the bridge between the institutional and the natural: between us and the rest of nature.

Always learning, never getting it right

A myth of nature, as we have seen, provides its holder with a way of seeing the world and with a way of not seeing it. This means that, if the world happens not to be the way the myth holder is convinced it is, he or she will not notice this discrepancy straight away. Enlightenment, therefore, is always time lagged and, since it results in the enlightened one being tipped out of one quadrant of the cultural theory scheme and into one of the other three, it comes as something of a shock: a surprise. Surprise, in other words, is always relative, which explains why, whenever something unexpected befalls us, there is always someone who saw it coming! The theory of surprise (Thompson and Tayler, 1986; Thompson *et al*, 1990) is built on this relativistic, but far from unconstrained, foundation:

- an event is never surprising in itself;

- it is potentially surprising only in relation to a particular set of convictions about how the world is;

- it is actually surprising only if it is noticed by the holder of that particular set of convictions.

For instance, an individualist, whose myth assures him that an ecosystem is so robust that it will recover from any perturbation, will be surprised when it collapses catastrophically. Similarly, a hierarchist, who is convinced that all ecosystems can be managed with predictable results, will be surprised when this turns out to be untrue. Conversely, an egalitarian, who believes that nature is precarious, will be surprised when those who have disregarded precautions do not reap the expected disaster. And a fatalist will be surprised if benefits, which he expects to be randomly distributed, continue to arrive.

Thus, surprises may be either pleasant or unpleasant, and a never ending sequence from one myth of nature to another may be proposed. Though all twelve transitions (see Figure 5.2) are possible, and we cannot say for sure what their order will be, we can spin a story to help us understand what is going on by privileging one particular sequence of possible changes so as to generate the socio-cultural analogue of Holling's ecocycle.[75]

- Let us start with Nature Benign. In this state of the world there is an excess of opportunity over existing investment, and this state, when interrogated by the myriad actions of individual agents, results in a positive-sum game in which (as Adam Smith famously put it) a hidden hand keeps adding to the welfare of the totality. As long as the excess continues (that is, as long as there is no rim to the deep basin that contains the ball), and learning by experimentation continues, we have the state of affairs assumed by *neoclassical economics*.

- But, as they say in show business, "Nothing recedes like success" and eventually exploitative behaviour causes the upper edge of the basin to turn downwards: Nature Perverse/Tolerant. The excess, for some actors, has now vanished. Transaction costs rise steeply, innovation brings losses more often than profits, and markets fail. This is the transition from markets to hierarchies described by the *new institutional economics* (Williamson, 1975).

- Hierarchically sustained transactions, in their turn, transform the environment that ushered them in; the "pocket of stability" gets shallower and shallower (making the system ever more *brittle*, as Holling puts it) and eventually the pocket of stability implodes: Nature Capricious. Both hierarchy and individualism (which has, of course, survived in the pocket) now lose their transactional grip and the world becomes a confusing, contradictory and unpredictable place: a place of which the fatalist's attitude; "Why bother?" makes perfect sense. There seems not to be an economic theory to go with this state of affairs, but the *theatre of the absurd* fits it quite nicely. How the world really is is wildly and irremediably out of line with how

---

75 If the reader refers back to Figure 3.4 she will see that this "sociocycle" exactly matches the sequence of transitions that constitutes the hermit's myth: Nature Resilient.

we could possibly imagine it to be. The playwright Samuel Beckett, once discharged from hospital after being stabbed in a Paris bar, sought out the person who had done it and asked him why. "How should I know?" came the reply!

- This flatland, however, is less hostile to those small, egalitarian and self-disciplined groups that strive to bring their needs down within what they perceive to be Mother Nature's frugal limits, and these groups are therefore well placed to take advantage (though that is not quite the right word) of the recessive realities that are about to overwhelm the conventional institutional arrangements: the hierarchies and the markets.

- In this next stage, Nature Ephemeral, all increases in scale bring punitive diseconomies, and the economy (like the universe that contains it) winds down and down. The *entropy principle* (Georgescu-Roegen, 1971) and the dictum *small is beautiful* (Schumacher, 1973) make economic sense here.[76] Yet, no matter how lightly everyone treads on the Earth, the ball eventually rolls down the slope, coming to rest in some other basin (Nature Benign) and we are back where we began: in a positive sum world that rewards the bold and skilful and that brings increasing returns to those who are prepared to act expansively.

Throughout this process, changes in the environment result from the actions of those whose strategy happens to be best suited to making the most of the environment in which they find themselves. As more and more of these strategists act, these endogenous changes accumulate, and the environment passes over a threshold into a state better suited to one of the other strategies, *ad infinitum*. Though this complex model may start at the same place as the simple one and have some of the same dynamics, its paths are infinitely more surprising and unpredictable. In this inherently complex system, in which ecological and socio-cultural

---

76   As, to some extent, does the more recently developed *ecological economics* with its efforts to internalize what are called "ecosystem services to man". But deep ecologists would see this as still too anthropocentic, urging instead that the focus should be on ecosystem functions: if you don't protect (and, where needed, restore) those there will not *be* any ecosystem services.

components interact, each myth of nature captures some aspects of the world at some time. But no one of them is ever right all the time and everywhere, and this means that each has its vital part to play. Clumsy institutions nurture that vitality; elegant ones destroy it.

CHAPTER 7

Surprise and its Invisible College

Surprise, in providing the crucial link between the one world we all inhabit and the different worlds we construct for ourselves (and thereby opening the way to a unified theory of man and nature) allows me to connect cultural theory with some other approaches which, though they do not originate from within anthropology, are saying much the same thing. Surprise, I have discovered, provides a meeting-ground for inquisitive minds from a wide range of disciplines: anthropology, production engineering, theoretical ecology, economics, ethology and, most interesting of all, given our present focus, organisation theory. So the gulf that separates those who insist that there is no such thing as an organisation from those who are content to define management as "management within an organisation" does not map straight onto the disciplinary distinction between anthropology and management science. The battle-line is more sinuous than this with, on one side, this invisible college that is gathered around the question of surprise and, on the other side, the parent disciplines of all those who have strayed across into this invisible college.[77]

Making invisible colleges visible, unfortunately, is a lengthy business and, even if I had the time, I would not be sufficiently competent in these fields to fully explain what is going on in them. Let me therefore resort to a little name-dropping: a few markers to give just an indication of these approaches and of how they begin to fit together.[78] And I can find these names by asking whether any others, besides cultural theorists, have come up with sociocycles that are roughly isomorphic with Holling's ecocycle. Indeed they have.

---

77 A fairly representative slice of this invisible college is conveniently assembled in Clark and Munn (1986), particularly the contributions by Holling, Timmerman, Brooks and Thompson.

78 In this section I am relying heavily on Tayler *circa* 1986.

- Utterback and Abernethy (1975) have proposed a three-stage *product life cycle*: a dynamic model of the process by which a product comes into existence, matures and eventually declines or is superseded. Each of these stages, they argue, is accompanied by a particular pattern of social relationships that renders it viable. In the early, technologically innovative, stage there is a high degree of "openness": highly-skilled personnel work in an informal way, creative thinking is valued, and such formal organisation as there is remains flexible and small in scale. After a time, the directions of demand and product development become clearer, and technological opportunities are more easily spotted and responded to in a way that becomes more and more "routine". This, of course, is only a transitional stage: a half-way house along the complexification process which eventually leads to a large-scale, vertically-integrated and rule-bound structure, within which innovation steadily gives way to cost reduction. The three stages, in other words, correspond to the classic transition from the anarchic competition of the r-selected species to the ordered whole of the climax community. But is that the end of the road?

- Ulanowicz (1979 and 1980), who has generalised the argument to biological and socio-economic systems, believes that it is, but the logic of the product life cycle itself (not to mention its name!) suggests otherwise. As the cycle carries both the hardware (the physical form of the production system) and the software (the interrelated people who made the production system work) further and further up-scale, and into ever greater interdependence and specialisation, the whole "organism" begins to lose strategic flexibility within the even larger system of which it is part: the market sector or the industry. The illusion of increasing control over its external environment then lures the whole lumbering beast to its ultimate demise. And this, when it comes, is sudden and devastating: an unanticipated "whole system" effect. The rest of this sociocycle, unfortunately, is not traced out by the theorists of product life, but at least this inevitable collapse of the mature product-and-production-system suggests that things *do* keep on changing.

- However, for devotees of *Kondratieff waves* (50-odd year economic ups-and-downs) this massive collapse is crucial; without it their vast historic cycles could not exist. I need to tread carefully here, because opponents of the whole idea of "long waves" insist that these sorts of cycles do not exist.[79] However, the objections are mostly to do with the claimed periodicity rather than with the sequence of stages that, it is hypothesised, constitutes the cycle itself. After all, there is nothing in Holling's ecocycle that says how fast or regular it will be; it is the stages, the order in which they come and the nature of the transitions between them that matter.[80] Similarly, if there is a sociocycle built upon a particular sequence that has become privileged (has become more likely, that is) thanks to the way in which we find ourselves caught up in our technologies - in our products, that is, and in the systems that produce them - then it is the stages, and not their timings, that deserve our attention. If a train keeps on arriving back where it started, the fact that it tends to follow the same route, out of the hundreds that are available to it, is of much more interest than whether it manages to arrive on time each time!

---

79   See Freeman (1993) for a survey of the proponents and the sceptics. Proponents have a good case when they point out that, regardless of whether the cycles themselves exist, interest in cycles is certainly cyclical. Moreover, as they point out with some glee, interest in cycles reaches a low at just the moment when that sort of understanding is most needed.
- "It is obvious that we are through with business cycles as we have known them" [The President of the New York Stock Exchange, September 1929]
- "The single most important tool in economic forecasting" [Joseph Schumpeter's verdict (1939) on Nikolai Kondratieff's model of long economic cycles].
- "There are very few ideas in macroeconomics that serious economists agree on, but doubting the existence of the Kondratieff is one of them" [Allen Meltzer, professor of political economy and public policy at Carnegie-Mellon University, quoted in Angrist (1991)].
   I am indebted to Robert Prechter for these quotations.

80   Timing (but relative, not absolute) is not irrelevant, since these transitions require two dynamics - a fast one that induces the strategy appropriate to the local attractor, and a slower one that, in transforming the global landscape of which the local attractor is one feature, gives rise to the strategy shifts that constitute the cycle itself - and the former does have to be faster than the latter.

Turning it all around the other way, I would say that if the cultural theory hypothesis is valid, and if our involvement with products does somehow privilege certain of the transitions that that hypothesis says are possible, then we would *expect* to see the sorts of economic oscillations that are called Kondratieff waves. We would not expect to see them everywhere in history, but we would expect to see them (and in fairly rapid succession) over the past two to three hundred years or so (because it is during that period that our involvement, both with products and with the outfits - firms - that generate those products, has been most intense).

The Kondratieff wave has four distinct phases: *exploitation* (fuelled by recent technological advances), *system crowding* (as more and more of the opportunities are taken up), *shake-out* (as retrenchment and rationalisation take hold) and *new possibilities* (arising, phoenix-like, from the wreckage of the preceding order). The stage is then set for the next Kondratieff, beginning with the exploitation of these new possibilities. These four phases, we can see, nicely match the ecocycle's progress: exploitation, climax community, creative destruction, and retention/mobilisation. Nor is this all.

- Cultural theory, in allowing us to ignore the time it takes to go round the cycle and to focus instead on the particular sequence of transitions that defines the Kondratieff, connects this sociocycle to a whole array of fourfold typologies: Astley and Van der Ven's (1983) classification of organisational theories, Burrell and Morgan's (1979) "meta-theory" of organisation, Elster's (1983) categorisation of economic theories of innovation, Ansoff's (1978) analysis of long-range planning methods, Namenwirth's (1973) and Weber's (1981) "preoccupational clusters" that keep on recurring both in the party platforms of United States presidential elections and in British Speeches from the Throne, and Kolb's (1976) and Fripp's (1982) "problem solving styles". The list could go on, into even more exotic terrain - Young's (1976) "geometry of meaning", Aristotle's four causes, Jung's (1964) "mandala", Mitroff, Kilmann and Barabba's (1977) "inquiring systems" and Graham Douglas' (1981) "radical astrology" - but it is already long enough for present purposes, which are to tease out the connections between some of the members of this invisible college that is struggling to identify all the vital and turbulent currents that exist beneath the deceptively calm organisational surface.

My argument, of course, is that all these fourfold (and cyclical) insights click together once they are confronted with cultural theory's four ways of organising (and with the hermit's subsumation of these four ways). However, there is another framework - actually from within organisation theory - which, it seems to me, is also capable of performing this integrative role. This is Emery and Trist's (1965) theory of the different environments that would be needed to support the organisational forms (or organisms) that we see existing all around us.

Emery and Trist arrive at a fourfold typology of the "causal texture of environments", the word "causal" referring to the organisational form (or organism) that each of these environments shapes. In other words, the assumption is that it is not what is inside the organism that matters but what the organism itself is inside of. The labels they give to these causal environments - "placid, randomised", "placid, clustered", "disturbed, reactive", and "turbulent" - are too compressed to provide immediate revelation but, once they are expanded a little, their identity with cultural theory's four myths of nature becomes much clearer. What also becomes clear is that Emery and Trist's theory, as with cultural theory, is a theory of *organisational learning*.

- *Placid, randomised.* In this environment noxiants (opportunities for learning from your mistakes) and goals (opportunities for learning from your successes) are randomly distributed. The complete absence of pattern as it moves through this environment means that the organism has no means (and cannot acquire any means) of knowing in advance what general course of action is best. Strategy is impossible; the best it can achieve are some short-term tactics for coping with a world in which sometimes things go its way, sometimes they do not, and there is no way of telling which it is likely to be. Learning does not increase the chance of survival and smallness is no disadvantage.

- *Placid, clustered.* There is some order in this environment, with noxiants tending to cluster with noxiants and goals with goals. Since the frequency with which an organism gets things wrong and gets things right varies as it moves through its environment, it is now able to learn something about the order that exists outside it. Nor is this learning just possible; it is helpful as well. There is the possibility of developing a strategy, and there is survival value in becoming a goal-seeking organism. Nothing, in this environment, succeeds like success!

- *Disturbed, reactive.* This environment is sufficiently crowded for each organism's environment to be made up, in quite large part, of all the other organisms. This means that it is no longer enough to follow the strategy that guarantees success in the straightforward *placid, clustered* environment; you have also to "second-guess" the other organisms. Operational planning (manoeuvring for position) emerges as another vital component between tactics and strategy. In other words, learning now has to be deeper: it has to extend to the rules that underlie the behaviour of the whole environment. What is right for one organism may not be right for another; it all depends on what positions have already been taken up.

- *Turbulent.* Here the complexities of the *disturbed, reactive* environment are continually augmented by the processes that the interactions between the organisms set off in the environment itself. Turbulence, in other words, is the result of the complexity of the interactions, those interactions being themselves shaped by tactics, strategies and operational planning techniques. Where the *placid, clustered* and *disturbed, reactive* environments favour large organisms, this environment offers no such advantage. The interconnectedness of everything undermines the adaptability that large organisms enjoy in less structured situations, because the adaptations they make are immediately fed through into even larger changes in their environment.

Total system collapse is built into the highly interconnected *turbulent* environment, and Emery and Trist actually draw on May's mathematics to support their idea that this combination of large and well-informed organisms interacting with, and changing, their environment cannot go on indefinitely. They expect the *placid, randomised* environment to follow this collapse, just as Holling sees compost as the immediate outcome of the creative destruction that befalls the climax community.[81] And, once this transition has happened, and all the large and complex organisms have been replaced by very small and simple ones, the logical progression through the *placid, clustered* and *disturbed, reactive* environments (both of which encourage small and simple organisms to get larger and more complex) is more or less assured.

So Emery and Trist's organism (which can be either a biological creature or a production unit made up of both inanimate "hardware" and animate "software") brings a particular momentum to all the interactions, thereby privileging just one sequence out of the vast number that this fourfold typology permits. This sequence, of course, is the hermit's myth (Nature Resilient) and we see it made manifest in Holling's ecocycle, in the product life cycle, in Kondratieff waves and, I venture, in pretty well any organised thing that we care to look at!

But that is enough of the invisible college. It is time I got back to the task I set myself a few chapters back: answering the seven questions that a theory of organising that denies there are such things as organisations must answer.

Five Questions Answered, Two To Go

To recapitulate the argument so far; the first three questions - "What are the ways of organising?", "How many of them are there?" and "Why just these ones?" - are answered by cultural theory's typology, together with its impossibility theorem. And for good measure, I have tried to drive home the impossibility theorem's message by exploring the various (but

---

81   There is, in fact, some doubt as to which way Holling sees things going after the collapse of the climax community. In some of his writing he has the small-scale fence-builders interposed between the climax community and compost. What really matters however is the fourfold typology, not the sequences that may or may not be privileged (see Price and Thompson, 1996).

far from infinite) ways in which we can become caught up in patterns of relationships that are both experienceable and shareable (the California condition).

The preceding discussion of surprise, and of the various non-anthropological theories that come together around that topic, has now answered two more of my seven questions - "What leads a person to embrace one way rather than another?" and "Can people change from one way to another?" Emery and Trist's "causal textures of the environment" explain how it is that patterns and dividuals support one another (in one case out of four) and fail to support one another (in the other three cases). This, of course, is their way of stating, in very general terms, the founding notion of cultural theory: that the individual is inherently relational. The question "Can people change from one way to another, and if so how does this happen?" is answered, very strongly, by cultural theory's rejection of the static/dynamic dualism: change becomes a necessary condition for the existence of the five destinations that make change possible. The second part of this question prompted me to open up the whole business of surprise (along with the idea of man and nature as a single but complex system) and to embark on the lengthy detour via the invisible college that I have just completed. If the world is out of kilter with your convictions as to how it is then, sooner or later, you are going to be dislodged from the pattern of social relations that has, as it were, supplied you with those convictions.

So there are just two questions left to answer: "How do the different ways of organising interact?" and "How do they manage to go on and on co-existing?" Let me open up this conundrum - interaction with neither extinction nor convergence - by way of a famous fourfold scheme that, up till now, I have managed not to mention: the "four-function paradigm" - *Adaptation, Goal-gratification, Integration* and *Latent pattern maintenance* (AGIL is the acronym) - that is the heart of Parsonian sociology.[82]

---

82 This is the structural-functional approach that was so ambitiously elaborated in the 1950s and 60s, by Talcott Parsons in particular, and which, with the subsequent rise of various schools of post-structuralism, has largely sunk from view. More's the pity, though the approach, as we will see, is not unflawed.

I will duck out of explaining what these four functions are, and how any social system (and, indeed, even a central heating system; see Tayler *circa* 1986) can be analysed in terms of them,[83] and just say that this typology, as originally stated by Parsons, Bales and Shils (1953), fits well with cultural theory and with all the other fourfold transitions I have mentioned. The right question was asked - "What are the preconditions for organisation?" - and the right answer was given - "A fourfold heterogeneity". Things went wrong, however, when it came to deducing the properties of the dynamical system that would keep this fourfold set of recurrent regularities in existence. In those days, the understanding of complexity (so far as it existed at all) was nothing more than a mathematical oddity,[84] and the notion of self-organisation was assumed to be part and parcel of the processes associated with dynamic equilibria (a market, for instance, self-organised - hidden hands and all that - because, so the assumption ran, there was a global equilibrium there for it to home-in on). Consequently, it is not surprising that Parsons, Bales and Shils assumed that their system was, as they put it, "self-equilibrating", and that the four functions they had correctly identified were functional for the totality - the entire social system - and not one for each of the divergent ways of organising that constituted that totality.

Cultural theory, by contrast, insists that the totality is a *dis*equilibrium system: a system in which the rival ways of organising are in perpetual and very far from balanced contention: endlessly trying to chew bits off one another, so as to strengthen their patterns and weaken the rival patterns. It is this idea of the *ceaseless predation* of the parts ensuring the coherence of the whole that is the key to the remaining two questions.

How Do They Coexist and Interact?

At the same time that the five ways of organising are in competition for adherents, so too, cultural theory insists, are they dependent on one another. Each way of organising ultimately needs each of its rivals, to

---

83   But see chapter 10 of Thompson, Ellis and Wildavsky (1990).

84   "Cantor dusts", for instance, have a long history. See Gleick (1987).

make up for its deficiencies, or to exploit, or to define itself against. Discernible difference in other words, is a precondition for cognition. Hence the postmodernist insight that to destroy the other is to murder the self. Were egalitarians to eliminate hierarchists and individualists, for instance, their lack of a target to be against would remove the justification for their strong group boundary (their closure and their strong connectedness) and thus undermine their solidarity. Or, to take another example, were individualists ever to rid the world of hierarchy, there would be no extra-market authority to enforce the laws of contract, thus producing the breakdown of the form of solidarity to which they are committed. Nor could fatalists be fatalistic if there were no hierarchies to exclude them, no individualists to pre-empt their personal network-building, and no egalitarian groups to demand levels of commitment they could never muster. And hermits could not withdraw into their hermitude if there were no coercive patterns of relationships for them to withdraw *from*.

This, more formally stated, is cultural theory's *requisite variety condition*: if one way of organising is there they will all be there. Conversely, if one of them goes into extinction they will all go into extinction. But this is not to say that all five ways of organising will be equally represented within a single country, or corporation or whatever. Indeed the fact that the whole thing is a disequilibrium system makes this a very *un*likely state of affairs. So how *do* the coexisting ways of organising interact? Though I feel that this is a question that is best investigated empirically, cultural theory can give a very general answer: they interact by ganging up on one another. Any two ways of organising can form an uneasy alliance. All it requires is that they foreground the things they have in common and background the things that set them apart.

- "American exceptionalism", for instance, in bringing individualism and egalitarianism together, has conspired to weaken hierarchy. In Britain, by contrast, hierarchy and individualism have allied in such a way as to largely exclude egalitarianism. Fatalism, of course, is not absent from these two regimes but it is not a component in the dominant alliance. In the former Soviet Union, however, it was the alliance of fatalism with hierarchy that gave the cold shoulder to both individualism and egalitarianism. ("We pretend to work and they pretend to pay us".) And, as the recent collapse of the Soviet Union has made clear, no regime - no pairwise alliance of solidarities - can go on for ever.

• Large corporations (to move down-scale socially) face outwardly towards markets but, internally, are strongly hierarchical. Too strongly, many now feel: hence all the recent efforts to introduce "intrapreneuring" and Total Quality. Fatalism and egalitarianism, of course, are present as well, but they are side-lined by the dominant alliance of hierarchy and individualism. But, when we look at some of the newer firms that have sprung up in response to the "green consumer" - alternative energy systems, waste treatment and recycling, boutique breweries, organic food and wine - we find that individualism is being allied with egalitarianism and that it is hierarchy that is being largely excluded.

• If we refer these examples to Ney's refurbishment of the classic theory of pluralist democracy (see Figure 1.5) we can see that they all manage not to learn lessons that, if only they had had more in the way of access or of responsiveness or of both, they could have learned. And in the book *Clumsy Solutions For A Complex World* (Verweij and Thompson 2006) we take this simple insight - the desirability of moving away from elegance and towards clumsiness - and apply it to a number of gripping tales of success and failure: Russia's botched transition to a market economy, the gun control stalemate in the US, seatbelt legislation around the world (to mention some of the elegant failures); novel water tariffs in California that are designed around the householders' plural ideas of fairness, small-to-medium hydro-power installations in the Himalaya and the Internet (to mention some of the clumsy successes).

These few examples, as well as providing the answer to the last of the seven questions, have allowed me to give a glimpse into the sort of ways in which such a theory can actually be brought to bear on the sorts of outfits that organisation theorists are interested in looking at. In other words, there *is* a theory of organisation that avoids the fallacy of misplaced concreteness, and it *can* be applied.

Closure At Last

In concentrating on impossibility theorems, requisite variety conditions, invisible colleges and the like I have neglected to explain just how it is that each of the myths of nature upholds just one of the ways of organising. Since this *unique functionality condition* - one myth, one pattern of social relations - is crucial to the operation of the disequilibrium system I have been describing, let me give a few examples to show that it is indeed valid. [It may be helpful here to refer back to Figures 2.1, 3.1, 3.2, 3.3 and 3.4.]

- An individualist who came to believe that nature was ephemeral (ball on an up-turned basin) could hardly justify the continuous process of trial-and-error that is the essence of his market way of life. If errors are essential to this solidarity (and they are) then the solidarity itself will have to go, because any little error will be likely to cause irreparable harm, not just to the person who makes it (which is the worst that can happen if nature is benign), but to everyone.

- A hierarchist who came to believe, with individualists, that there was no limit on what nature could take would no longer see any purpose in having experts to determine exactly where those limits lie. On top of that, if those limits (and the regulations by which their respect is enforced) were to disappear (as they would if no-one supported the experts) there would be no way of keeping the different ranks of humankind (in this case, expert and lay) separate from one another. Status differences would decay, symmetrical transactions would displace asymmetrical ones, and Schmutzer and Bandler's transaction matrix would cease to be "upper triangular".

- If egalitarians came to share the individualists' conviction that nature is benign, there would be so much of everything valuable that there would be no point in sharing out. Since the scrupulous sharing out of the meagre and depleting resources Mother Nature has endowed us with is what the egalitarians' way of organising (closure and strong connectedness) is set up to do, that would be the end of it.

- If fatalists came to believe that there were patterns in nature, they would then realise that it was possible for them to get in sync with these predictable forces. And if they did that they could then do something to control their fate, in which case they would no longer be fatalists.

- If hermits granted the permanent validity of any one of the four "primary" myths, they would be insisting that the ball could go on and on moving through that particular landscape without ever affecting its contours. In other words, they would be denying the transformational properties of the system: the inevitability of each of the "engaged" ways of organising being undermined by the desires it kindles in those who support it. In failing to see through to the essential one-ness of existence, these hermits would be stopping the wheel of life and getting off at one or other of the stages it cycles through. Ignorance would have won over enlightenment, and they would have joined that which they had previously organised themselves against.

We can now see the essential message of these cultural theory diagrams, which is that only one myth of nature will support each pattern of social relationships. All the others would undermine that pattern. In other words, the upholders of a way of organising, in strengthening their preferred way, are *at the same time* weakening the rival ways. Hence each way of organising is also, four times over, a way of disorganising.

CHAPTER 8

Heinz Minus Seven:
The Fifty Varieties of Social Science

"Yes, but cultural theory is *just* a theory" is a put-down that I often run into, so let me pause here for a moment so as to get my retaliation in first. "Yes, of course it is just a theory", is my initial response, "but so too is Einstein's general theory of relativity, Darwin's theory of evolution, superstring theory, quantum theory, Wegener's theory of continental drift, Maxwell's kinetic theory of gases, and as many more as you care to add". Since we either have theories or we have nothing, to say that something is just a theory is to say precious little: bugger all, in fact.

What matters about a theory is how *good* it is. Darwin's theory of evolution, for instance, is generally judged to be pretty good, and even better once John Maynard Smith had filled in a rather gaping hole within it. (Darwin, faced with the fact that individual animals often did not behave as ruthlessly as they could, had resorted to an unexplained altruism: they hold back "for the good of the species". Smith [1982], drawing on mathematical game theory, which had not been around in Darwin's day, was able to show that this seemingly less-than-best strategy was in fact the best: "Nice guys come first!"[85]) So a first test of a theory, you could say, is whether it is dense and structured enough for you to be able to find holes in it. You could not do that with intelligent design, for instance.

Nor is this the only criterion for sorting out better and worse theories.

- Some, like that famous beer, refresh the parts other theories cannot reach; and cultural theory, as we have seen, enables us to expect behaviour - such as Greenpeace's thwarting of the Brent Spar's deep ocean disposal - that must always remain a surprise to those who are operating with any of the conventional twofold theories.

---

85   The strategy, being what game theorists call "uninvadeable", is evolutionarily stable, whilst the more ruthless strategies are not.

- Some theories can be judged better because they do more with less. For instance, cultural theory has been shown to provide a more parsimonious and more complete explanation of value changes than does the theory of post-materialism (Grendstad and Selle 1999).

- Some theories are more counter-intuitive than others: a characteristic that physicists, in particular, view as a definite plus (as in Wolfgang Pauli's verdict on an over-commonsensical theory: "It's so bad it isn't even wrong"). And cultural theory, in starting with the unobvious - the forms of social solidarity and not the individual - scores quite highly on this criterion (that cultural dynamics are independent of social scale is likewise counter-intuitive, as is the idea that micro and macro are each the cause of the other).

- Some theories are fundamentally irreconcilable with others, in which case we need to devise experiments, or gather evidence, that will help us decide between them. But each will need to be falsifiable for this to be possible; so falsifiability is also an important criterion for a good theory. Cultural theory, in predicting that a particular pattern of social relations will always accompany a particular social construction of nature, and that both, in their turn, will accompany a particular way of acting (a particular behavioural strategy) is eminently falsifiable - just one wrong accompaniment would be enough!

- But sometimes a theory, far from being irreconcilable with others, subsumes them as limited special cases. That, as we have seen with the markets-and-hierarchies framing for instance, is the case with cultural theory, and of course a subsuming theory is better than the subsumed theory (even though, as with relativity and Newtonian mechanics, the subsumed theory is often fine for many practical purposes).

- Some theories are more satisfying, aesthetically, than others. If they turn out not to be supported empirically we are likely to be disappointed, whilst an ugly theory will be thankfully discarded. Jevons' explanation for the trade cycle in terms of solar activity (the "sunspot cycle") was regretfully abandoned when it became apparent (a) that the two cycles were not properly in step[86] and (b) that the trade cycle's amplitude increased as the economic contribution of agriculture (the only sector likely to be affected by the sun's intensity) decreased. Indeed, theories of the trade cycle did not regain this sort of aesthetic level until the arrival of the Hansen-Samuelson model a century or so later (the intervening theories having invoked "floors" and/or "ceilings" to bounce back economic trends that otherwise would have continued on their downward or upward ways).

- Jevons' theory was *reductionist*, in that phenomena at the social level were explained in terms of what was going on at the physical level; the Hansen-Samuelson model, by contrast, was *endogenous*, the cycle being generated entirely through the interactions of the economic actors themselves (thanks to the inevitably time-lagged feedback of information about levels of demand). All of which suggests that reductionism is not necessarily the mark of a good theory. Cultural theory, of course, is wholly endogenous (unlike sociobiology, say, which is strongly reductionist).

- The fewer uncaused causes that are invoked by a theory the more likely it is to be judged a good one. The markets-and-hierarchies frame, for instance, explains a lot but it does not have anything to say about where markets and hierarchies themselves come from. Cultural theory, as we have seen, does (and, for good measure, completes the typology of forms of social solidarity whilst also explaining where those extra three forms come from, and why it is that there aren't any more).

- Closure - an absence of loose ends - is another mark of a good theory. An impossibility (or classification) theorem - a proof that, given certain explicit assumptions, the forms or recurrent regularities predicted by a theory are the only ones there could be - is a very definite plus. René Thom's (1972) specification of the various catastrophes that are possible (in

---

86   Or, rather, properly *entrained* (i.e. having the same period). The sunspot cycle has to anticipate the trade cycle, so as to give time for the thunderstorms that are caused by solar activity to affect the crop yields (and, to be pedantic, for the sun's heat to get here).

up to 4 dimensions) is a famous example that won him the Fields medal - mathematics' most distinguished award.[87] And Arrow's (1951/1963) impossibility theorem (about not being able to determine a best social choice from individual values) is a rare example from social science. So cultural theory, having an impossibility theorem - one, moreover, that sets off by ruling out Arrow's explicit assumptions, on the grounds that they deny the inherent relationality of the individual - is in rather select company.

No doubt this list of criteria for deciding how good a theory is could go on (dynamic theories, for instance, other things being equal, are better than static ones) but my point here is simply to show that cultural theory does rather well, at least by social science standards.[88] And, to drive this point home (and, I hope, skewer those who try to dismiss it as "just a theory") let me now quickly set out how well cultural theory does on just two of these criteria: *subsumation of other theories* and *closure*.

Blind Men and N-Dimensional Elephants

[In this section I am going to simplify things a little by leaving out the fifth solidarity - autonomy - and its social being: the hermit. Since few, if any, social theories make room for the hermit, and since I will be looking at cultural theory's ability to subsume those theories as special cases, this simplification seems justifiable, in the sense that, if a fourfold scheme can subsume them all there is no point in making it fivefold.]

One of the nice things about cultural theory's fourfold typology (i.e. the three active solidarities plus fatalism) is the way it sorts out the otherwise mutually incompatible framings that have been proposed by

---

87 Catastrophes are the various configurations of attractors and repellers that explain why it is that gradual changes along the "control dimension" sometimes give rise to sudden and discontinuous changes along the "behaviour dimension" (as, for instance, when the last straw breaks the camel's back). For a guided walk through Thom's classification theorem see Zeeman (1977, ch1).

88 Natural scientists who have taken the trouble to acquaint themselves with social science have come away quite shocked. Richard Feynman, for instance, likened it to a "cargo cult": it has all the trappings of proper science, but in the same way that the airstrips built by charismatic leaders in the New Guinea highlands have realistic radio aerials that turn out to be made of jungle vines!

"the masters". The legal historian, Sir Henry Maine, for instance, back in 1861, distinguished two forms of solidarity - he called them *status* and *contract* - and proposed a one-way historical transition from status to contract. In other words, we used all to be bound together in a "positional" and group-ordered way ("lower orders" and "upper echelons"); now we are all bound by individualistic "weak ties": one-to-one and mutually agreed relationships that can be ended by either party after any exchange. This celebrated distinction, with its one-way arrow, lives on in the oft-drawn contrast between *traditional* and *modern* (it is even implicit in *postmodernism*, since you cannot become postmodern if you have not managed to get yourself to modern!).

A quarter of a century later, the German sociologist Ferdinand Tönnies (1887) also drew a famous dualistic distinction - *Gemeinschaft* versus *Gesellschaft* - in which societies that are bound by ties of kinship, friendship and local tradition (societies about which Tönnies himself was very dewy-eyed) were contrasted with those that are animated by individualistic competition and (echoing Maine) contract. And six years later, the French anthropologist Emile Durkheim (1893) introduced the term "solidarity" through his even more famous dualistic distinction between *mechanical solidarity* (in which agents bind themselves to others on the basis of sameness) and *organic solidarity* (in which agents are bound together by the interdependence of specialised social roles). "Aha", you may cry, "three instances of that well-known phenomenon, independent discovery!"[89], but you would be wrong. Indeed you will probably go mad if you try to map these dualistic schemes onto one another. It simply cannot be done; at any rate, not without Procrustean amputations so disfiguring as to render some of them unrecognizable.

Cultural theory explains why. In Figure 8.1 each of these schemes is mapped onto the fourfold typology, and the source of the madness is graphically clear.

---

89 The rather large time-gaps being explained away by the fact that each discoverer was writing in a different language.

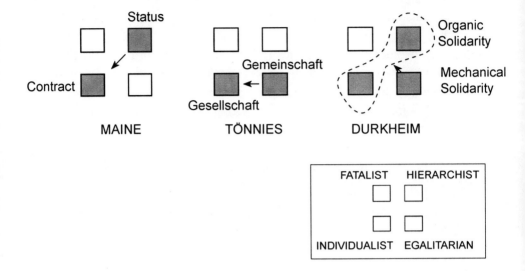

Figure 8.1: Mapping the Masters

- Maine, we can now see, has contrasted two of the four solidarities - hierarchy and individualism - and ignored the other two.

- Tönnies has contrasted egalitarianism and individualism, and then ignored the other two (though it could also be argued that he has uncritically merged egalitarianism and hierarchy and then contrasted that blob with individualism).

- Durkheim has contrasted some amalgam of individualism and hierarchy with egalitarianism, and ignored the other one.

- All three masculine masters have ignored fatalism, but it did not escape the notice of their contemporary, the industrial novelist Elizabeth Gaskell. The very title of her *North and South* (Gaskell 1855) hints at a dualistic scheme, and she does indeed begin by having her heroine move from the *Gemeinschaft* world of rural Hampshire to the *Gesellschaft* setting of Manchester's teeming mills and factories (though, unlike Tönnies, she is not at all dewy-eyed about the lost *Gemeinschaft*). Once "oop North", her attention (like that of her fellow Northerner, Engels) is soon drawn to those whose lives she describes as being "like a lottery", and this behavioural stance, quite clearly, is supportive of neither *schaft*. Indeed, you could say that these excludees have found themselves *schafted*; and it is that shared experience, together with the rational "What's the point?" behavioural response, that forms them into a solidarity: fatalism. Nor, interestingly, does she stop at three. Having married the impressively individualistic mill-owner, her heroine prevails on him to introduce a modest measure of hierarchy - a works dining room - thereby getting him to behave appropriately in relation to the status difference between him and his employees. Of course, Mrs Gaskell was not explicit about these four solidarities, but they are certainly there.[90] And her clumsy - four solidarity-respecting - solution, with which the book happily concludes, marks her out as the Grandmother of Cultural Theory (the Mother, of course, being Mary Douglas).

---

90   In much the same way that three of them are there in my Arsenal Football Club story. The fourth solidarity - fatalism - was also there (in its typically non-vocal way) in the form of the loyal and much put-upon local supporters. They, since they find their way by foot to the stadium, relying on favoured pubs and chip shops along the way, would have been at a complete loss if Arsenal had moved out of the borough.

I am not claiming any originality here - cultural theorists have been "mapping the masters" for the past 30 or so years[91] - but I would now like to show that there is another tack we can take. Instead of just fitting the various masters to the cultural theory scheme, we can ask a rather ambitious (but surprisingly easily answered) question: how many different fittings are possible - logically possible that is?

There are, it turns out, 50 different fittings: 50 different ways of getting the elephant not quite right.[92] And, of course, the dualistic schemes are less right than the trinitarian ones, and the unitarian ones (being most lacking in the requisite variety) are the least right of all. Figure 8.2 sets out all the dualistic schemes that are logically possible, and they are arranged in a number of groupings, according to the sorts of ignoring and/or merging

---

91 Mary Douglas, for instance, had Maine mapped in her lectures at University College London, back in the 1960s. Ostrander (1982) then roped in several more masters (some of them unitarians rather than dualists), and the momentum has since been maintained in various ways. Thompson, Ellis and Wildavsky (1990) mapped an even longer list of masters, Thompson and Rayner (1998) went back to our masculine trio, added some twentieth century descendents, and then teased out the underlying distinctions that gave them their dualistic but mutually incompatible schemes, and Verweij (2008) has scrutinized a long list of political scientists and theorists of international relations and sorted them out according to their identities and mutual incompatibilities (at present this is just a teaching aid - *Grid and Group Galore* [m.verweij@jacobs-university.de]). And so it goes; the wise men all getting hold of different bits of the fourfold elephant. Had any of them paused, at any time over the last century and a half, or even paid a little more attention to Elizabeth Gaskell, they could have compared what they had got hold of with what the others had got hold of and thereby found their way to cultural theory's fourfold scheme. But they didn't! All of which suggests that social science has not been anywhere near as scientific as it could have been: too much mutual disdain and not enough comparing and testing of rival theories.

92 That is with just the statics. The number increases severalfold, once we introduce the dynamics - the various arrows between the solidarities. Maine's twofold scheme, for instance, can be dynamised in two other ways. The historical arrow can be in the opposite direction to his one-way Maine Street from status to contract (as indeed it is in Hayek's [1944] "road to serfdom") and it can be a combination of these two (as it is in Williamson's (1975) "new institutionalism" (which, like Oxford's New College, is no longer *that* new). There are, of course, no dynamics in the unitarian schemes we will be coming to, whilst, at the other extreme, cultural theory, as we have seen, argues for the full complement of arrows within its fourfold scheme: 12, all of which can also be discerned in "real life" (see ch 4 of Thompson, Ellis and Wildavsky 1990).

principles that I have already drawn on in explaining the madness that closes in on those who try to map Maine onto Tönnies and so on (see Figure 8.1).

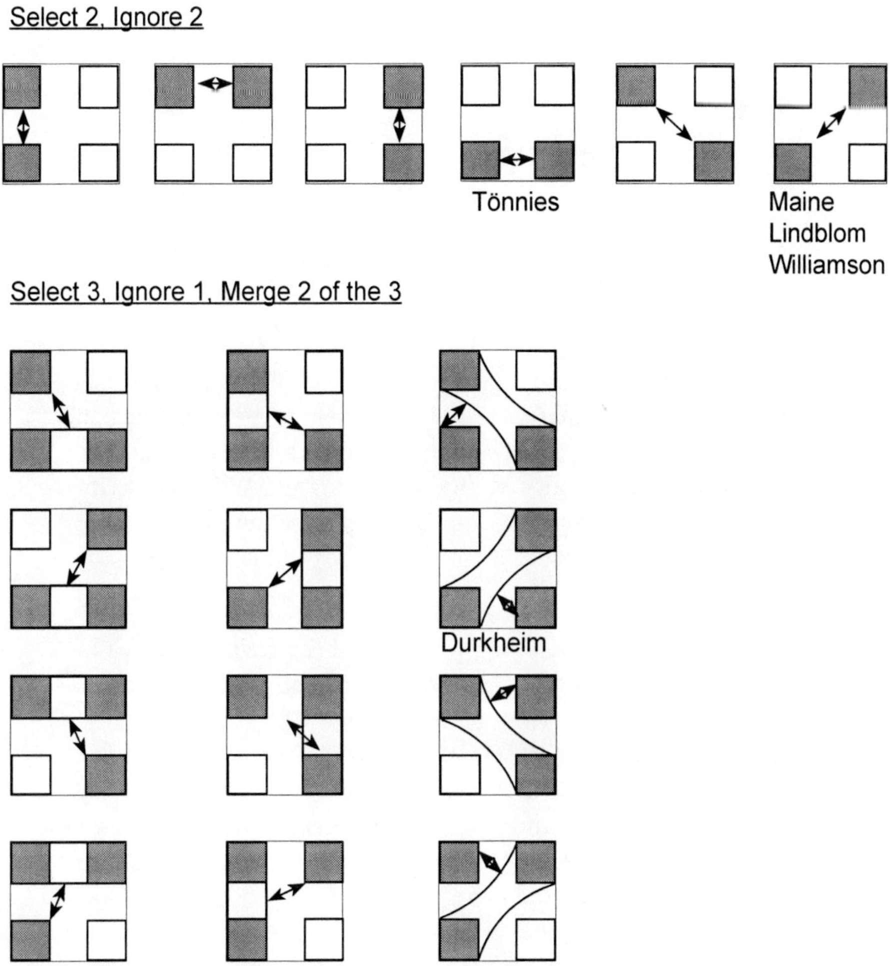

Select 2, Ignore 2

Tönnies

Maine
Lindblom
Williamson

Select 3, Ignore 1, Merge 2 of the 3

Durkheim

Figure 8.2: The 25 Possible Dualistic Schemes

Select 4, Merge 2x2

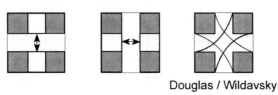

Douglas / Wildavsky

Select 4, Merge 3

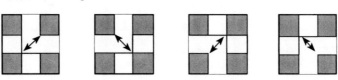

Figure 8.2 (cont): The 25 Possible Dualistic Schemes

- Wherever one of these logically possible dualisms corresponds to a mapping of a master I have noted that, and we can see that some dualisms have just one master, others have several, and still others none at all. Maine, Lindblom and Williamson, for instance, cluster together, though they separate out (to some extent) once one adds in the various dynamic options. (See Footnote 91.)

- A rather curious "inhabited" possibility is where the solidarities on each of the two diagonals are merged and then contrasted with one another. This actually comes from two cultural theorists - Douglas and Wildavsky (1982) - who, in their book *Risk and Culture*, ended up collapsing the fourfold scheme they had laboriously set out into a "stable diagonal" (individualism merged with hierarchy) and an "unstable diagonal" (fatalism merged with egalitarianism). This collapsed state of affairs - they called it "centre versus border" - can be achieved by striking out several of the 12 arrows in cultural theory's dynamicised typology (see Figure 5.2) - something that Mary Douglas (2005) has now conceded was not a valid thing to have done (since it ruled out certain interactions that have since been shown - by Gyawali [2001], for instance, and in my Arsenal Football Club story - to occur quite readily, often with some remarkably positive consequences: consequences that do not sit comfortably with the "unstable diagonal" label or with the "centre versus border" distinction). I mention all this, not to gloat, but in order to highlight one of cultural theory's remarkable properties: its ability to correct cultural theorists when, for all sorts of readily understandable reasons, they get things wrong (or, rather, not quite right).

- Another interesting feature (and this, we will see, also holds for the trinitarian and unitarian possibilities) is that quite a lot of them are "uninhabited": they have no master. This, among other perhaps more serious things,[93] raises some attractive new career options. An ambitious young social scientist, instead of writing yet another book on Weber or Durkheim or Marx, can now secure a fancy, named chair at some prestigious university by colonising one of these unoccupied possibilities.

Figure 8.3, following the same ignoring and/or merging principles, sets out all the trinitarian possibilities, of which there are 10.

Select 3, Ignore 1

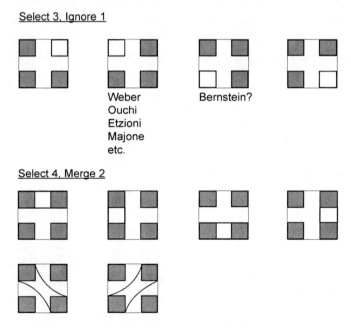

Weber
Ouchi
Etzioni
Majone
etc.

Bernstein?

Select 4, Merge 2

Figure 8.3: The 10 Possible Trinitarian Schemes

---

93   One of which is the likely invalidity of off-the-cuff rejections of any theoretical frameworks that are made from a position that demonstrably embraces less of the requisite variety than does the framework that is being rejected.

- There turns out to be a rather large cluster of masters (twentieth and twenty-first century ones) attached to just one of these 10: the one in which cultural theory's three "active" solidarities (individualism, hierarchy and egalitarianism) are clearly distinguished, whilst the fourth and somewhat "passive" one - fatalism - is ignored.[94] However, this would not be entirely fair to the social capital theorists, Szreter and Woolcock (2004), with their three kinds of social capital: *bonding* (which equates toegalitarianism), *bridging* (which equates to individualism) and *linking* (which equates to hierarchy). This is because social capitalists, even when, like Putnam (1993), they recognise only one form of social capital (in Putnam's case it seems to be bonding social capital), always contrast that positive (but undiscerning) state of affairs with the troublesome situation (from a development point of view) in which there is no social capital at all (which, of course, equates to fatalism). So Szreter and Woolcock, you can say, have actually got the requisite variety: the fourfold scheme. As yet, however, social capitalists have had little if anything to say about the dynamics (are the different kinds of social capital additive, or multiplicative, or do they wipe one another out, like matter and anti-matter?) and that, I would suggest, is where cultural theory can help them.

- I have tentatively attached to one of the other possibilities the socio-linguist Basil Bernstein (1971). He and Mary Douglas worked closely together in the 1970s, and believed themselves to be operating with the same typology. However, I had a terrible time when, in the course of my PhD, I tried to map their schemes onto one another. Indeed, I was only saved from the men in the white coats when, almost by chance, Bernstein admitted that one of his four quadrants was uninhabited (in contrast to Douglas', which were all well-stocked with social beings). This, I should stress, is a very tentative assignment, and it is quite likely that Bernstein has ended up doing something rather odd here: perhaps managing to divide one solidarity into two.

---

94   For a rather longer list see Thompson, Verweij and Ellis (2006). And for an even longer list, together with the claim that *all* institutional approaches now recognise these three forms of solidarity see Tilly (2006)

- So I hope it is now evident that master-mapping, even with the help of this complete set of possible fittings, is often a far from straightforward business. For instance, Dipak Gyawali (2000) has assigned the three forms of power in the Hindu scriptures to the already well-populated possibility - *tamasik* to hierarchy, *rajasik* to individualism and *satwik* to egalitarianism - but this has been queried by Catherine Lee (personal communication) who argues that *tamasik*, from her reading of the scriptures, equates to fatalism. Perhaps they are both right, in the sense that *tamasik* has uncritically merged hierarchy and fatalism (the first possibility in the second row in Figure 8.3). The point is, not that cultural theory can immediately resolve these sorts of disputes (unfortunately you cannot go and talk to the ancient Hindu sages in the way you can go and talk to Szreter and Woolcock) but simply that it makes it possible to have them.

And finally, Figure 8.4 sets out all the unitarian possibilities, of which there turn out to be 15. These possibilities, since (as I have already mentioned) they are the most lacking in the requisite variety, are the least right of all: less right than the dualistic schemes which, in turn, are less right than the trinitarian schemes. But (or perhaps I should say so) they are far and away the most popular among social scientists.

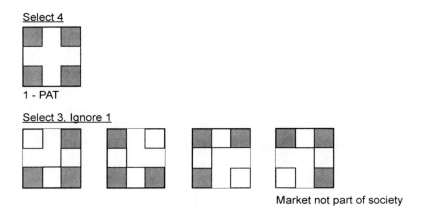

Figure 8.4: The 15 Possible Unitarian Schemes

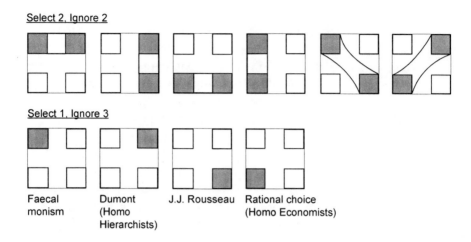

Select 2, Ignore 2

Select 1, Ignore 3

Faecal monism	Dumont (Homo Hierarchists)	J.J. Rousseau	Rational choice (Homo Economists)

Figure 8.4 (cont): The 15 Possible Unitarian Schemes

The immensely influential I-PAT formulation - that environmental Impact is some multiplication of Population, Affluence and Technology (Ehrlich and Holdren 1974) undiscerningly lumps all four solidarities into a single homogenized blob (the first possibility in Figure 8.4), thereby blinding itself to all the remarkably different kinds and levels of impact that each of the solidarities is likely to generate (the population, affluence and technological trajectories also vary markedly as we go from one solidarity to another, as is made very clear in what is called the perspectives approach to integrated environmental assessment [Rotmans and de Vries 1997]). Of course, things have to be uniform at the micro-level if you are doing the sort of "top down" computer modelling that is currently so relied on by policymakers: hence all those horrendously insensitive measures such as *national per capita consumption*, which is just one macro-number (national consumption) divided by another macro-number (national population). That might work for cows, out there on the range, but it is a hopelessly blunt instrument for understanding what humans are up to.[95]

---

95   For some quite detailed suggestions as to how such approaches (they go by
      the term *integrated assessment*) might transfer themselves from bluntness to
      sharpness see Thompson (1997).

- Many early theorists of social capital went to considerable lengths to exclude conventional capital - the kind that individualistic actors are intent on piling up - from their otherwise undiscerning notion of social capital (a position that fits with the last possibility in the first row of Figure 8.4). Indeed, this is just one instance of the prevalent assumption that the market, being an individualistic activity, is not social (as, for instance, in the oft-drawn distinction between *market incentives* and *social sanctions*). But, now that three distinct forms of social capital have been recognised, this absurdity has been corrected, with *bridging* social capital (the individualist form) being every bit as social as the rest.

- The last row ("Select 1, Ignore 3") is well populated. First, there is *faecal monism*: the fatalist conviction that the whole world is made of excrement (as in the German expression "Alles Scheisse!"). At number two we have Louis Dumont's (1972) *homo hierarchicus* (which those who do not share this particular mapping tend to dismiss as nothing more than an apology for the Hindu caste system). Rousseau's "Born free yet everywhere in chains" maps onto number 3, and last (but, in terms of worldly and academic influence, far and away first) we find *homo economicus*: that insatiable and self-seeking paragon who can be relied upon always to know his preferences and, moreover, to be able to rank them accurately.

- These 15 possibilities, as well as being the most impoverished in requisite variety terms, have no dynamics whatsoever. If there is only one place to be you can't go anywhere else, as Yogi Berra might have said.[96] So the unitarian possibilities really do represent the dismal depths, and the fact that so much of social science (and so much of the influence that social science has) is located down here is truly dispiriting. But, looking on the bright side, now that we have mapped all these possibilities, at least we have a better idea of where up is!

In conclusion, we can now see that there are, in all, 50 different ways of getting the elephant not quite right: 25 dualistic ways, 10 trinitarian

---

96   What he actually said was "If you don't know where you are going you may end up some place else".

ways and 15 unitarian ways, and we find giant figures in social science, along with their various influential theories, attached to some of the possibilities within each of these three classes. All very intriguing, but what does it mean?

- What we have here (in sketchy outline, admittedly) is a general theory of social science:[97] an elephantine theory, as it were, that accommodates all those more partial (i.e. limited special case) theories that, on the unitarian, dualistic or trinitarian views, are mutually contradictory. It is not saying that those theories that it accommodates are wrong (which is what each of them, in the absence of this subsuming theory, is saying about the others); only that none of them is entirely right. Each, it suggests, since there are 50 in all, is 2% right and 98% wrong.

- But we can be a little more discerning than this, in that a threefold scheme is surely less wrong than is a twofold one, and it, in turn, is surely less wrong than is a onefold one. Hence the downward journey to the dismal depths where most of social science, to its great discredit, is located.

- Since the number of possibilities - 50 in all - is higher than social scientists have hitherto entertained, there are (as I have already mentioned) a fair few that have no master attached to them. This is certainly a surprising discovery, but it is not immediately obvious what we should make of it (apart from that bit of fun about the new career opportunities that it opens up). On the one hand, if we accept the validity of this theory of theories, and move ourselves across to the fourfold scheme that subsumes the other 50 as limited special cases, it really does not matter whether or not they come with attached masters. On the other hand, disciplines and schools, being strongly path-dependent, are unlikely to just hop across like this onto the subsuming theory; they can be counted on to dig in their toes, each in the particular special case possibility that it has made itself so dependent on. So there is the intriguing question of "paths not taken". What, we can now ask ourselves, would

---

97   More properly perhaps, a "classification theorem" that provides us with a theory
      of social science theories: both those that have been expounded and those that,
      though equally feasible, happen to have not yet been expounded.

the various disciplines and schools that we have not got look like, had we happened to entrench ourselves in the various "uninhabited" possibilities to the same sorts of extents that we *have* entrenched ourselves in the ones that do happen to have become inhabited?

- The writing of ramblers' guides to these paths not taken, clearly, could become a major PhD industry, and a valuable means of delivering the "optimal perturbations" needed to jolt current disciplines and schools out of their various ruts. But a word of warning is in order. Some of these uncolonised niches, though logically distinct, may in practice be hard to distinguish from others (and that includes the inhabited ones). Common tree-creepers and short-toed tree-creepers, to draw on ornithological analogy, *are* separate species, but you would need to have one in each hand, and an opened field guide in front of you, to actually tell them apart! For instance, the unitarian approach that lumps all four solidarities together as hierarchical (say) will not be easily distinguished from one that zeroes in on hierarchy and ignores the other three. But perhaps not (the former, for instance, is likely to be strongly normative; the latter less so), these sorts of subtle distinctions not having been looked at at all yet. How could they have been, in the absence of this theory of theories that makes these sorts of subtle distinctions evident?

- The handle that this theory of theories gives us on all the path-dependency and mutual disdain that so bedevil social science is a fresh, and potentially constructive, take on the sorts of acrimonious disputes that are so characteristic of social science. One such dispute has recently blown up around the prestigious Journal of The American Political Science Association, the editorial policy of which has been captured by just one of the 15 unitarian possibilities (number 4 in the last row in Figure 8.4). The result has been the out-of-hand rejection of papers from any of the other 49 possibilities: hardly a step in the direction of scientific progress! This theory of theories would enable that journal's editorial board to be a little more circumspect about what they reject, and how. But path-dependency, as my final example makes clear, should not be under-estimated.

- One senior, and intemperate, professor of international relations - a neo-realist (demonstrably one of the 15 unitarian possibilities) - has dismissed cultural theory as "bizarre", and has forbidden his doctoral students to use it. That is behaviour that should (and, now that we have this 50-component scheme, can) be challenged. Moreover, the challenge can be particularly strong in this case because of the two schemes' positions in the "pecking order". Refutations of threefolders by those who are themselves twofolders should be treated with a measure of scepticism, and refutations of fourfolders by those who are themselves onefolders (which is what we have here) deserve to be treated with an even larger measure of scepticism.

More discernment within the social science profession and less apoplexy among its practitioners are therefore just two of the practical benefits of this theory of theories. None of which, of course, means that it is true. Cultural theory, though a good theory, *is* just a theory.

CHAPTER 9

Cultural Theory Without Grid and Group

My aim, over the preceding chapters, has been to set out cultural theory in such a way as to interest, and challenge, those (organisation theorists, new institutionalists, management scientists and so on) who concern themselves with the study of institutions. But in doing this I have done something which those who are already familiar with cultural theory will find surprising and, perhaps, shocking. From start to finish I have made no mention whatsoever of "grid" and "group": the two "dimensions of sociality" that constitute the very heart of most previous expositions of cultural theory. A word or two of explanation is in order.

Mary Douglas, the founder of cultural theory, always insisted that her invention is not in fact a theory; just an "analytical scheme" or an "heuristic device". The device - "grid:group analysis", as she called it - is a way of measuring a person's "social context": a way, in other words, of getting to grips with the crucial variations in the inherent relationality of the individual. Two dimensions, she argued, are needed: *group*, which is defined as "the experience of a bounded social unit", and *grid*, which refers to the "rules that relate one person to others on an ego-centred basis" (Douglas, 1970, p.viii). Then, by distinguishing just two positions on each dimension: "strong" and "weak"[98] - she generated the four *social beings/forms of solidarity* that constitute the basic typology from which everything else follows:

---

98   Or sometimes "high" and "low".

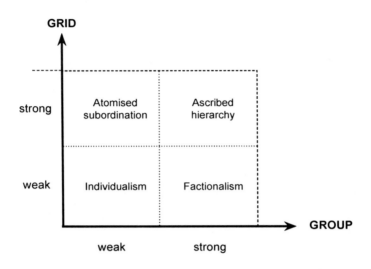

GRID

strong | Atomised subordination | Ascribed hierarchy

weak | Individualism | Factionalism

weak | strong | **GROUP**

Figure 9.1: Grid and Group (based on Douglas 1982, p.4)

Douglas's typology, clearly, is the same as the one I have developed (except that it is fourfold, not fivefold), and her dimensions of grid and group are clearly getting hold of much the same distinctions as I have used in sorting out the different experienceable patterns of social relationships, but there are no *dynamics* here. So the big question, if this analytical scheme works (and there is now ample evidence that it does), is "What would be the simplest dynamical system that would generate the recurrent regularities that are captured by this typology?" This is the question that a theory, as opposed to an analytical scheme, will have to answer.

This, of course, is the question I have asked, and answered, in the preceding chapters. If cultural theory looks strange (and it *does* look strange to many social scientists) it is because it is answering a question that not everyone has got round to asking yet. And the great achievement of Douglas' analytical scheme (above and beyond its instrumentality: it *does* work[99]) is that it makes it more difficult for us not to ask this question.

---

99   There is a bibliography of cultural theory, including many examples of its application, in Thompson, Ellis and Wildavsky (1990).

Yet, for all its achievements, this analytical scheme is not without its problems.

- What happens in the middle? Is there a "grey mish-mash", or does a tiny shift from one side of a dotted line to the other result in a category jump whilst a much bigger shift that stays within a single box result in no change at all?

- What about the hermit? Is there not some way of avoiding doing what Douglas has had to do: take the hermit "off the social map"?

- What is the unit of analysis? Is it the individual (in which case that individual's social involvement must all take place in just one compartment) or is it the pattern of social relationships (in which case an individual may lead different parts of his or her life in different compartments)?

- Are the two dimensions really orthogonal? Might it be that a move up grid, say, inevitably entails a corresponding shift along the group dimension? In other words, perhaps the two dimensions are simply serving to plot a range of positions along some diagonal: a diagonal that, had it been properly identified, would have captured all the variation in terms of just a single dimension.

Since these problems stem from certain shortcomings of the analytical scheme itself - its lack of any dynamical system to generate the typology, its use of continuous dimensions to depict discontinuous patterns (*topologies*, as Manfred Schmutzer calls them) and so on - they cannot be resolved by reference to that analytical scheme. And this debilitating circularity, over the years, has resulted in many people being turned off by the very scheme that first attracted them. That is why we need a *theory*, and that is why I have not mentioned grid and group.

The Simplest Dynamical System

Transaction theory, as we have seen, provides a "homing-in mechanism" which ensures that as we transact with others we will be carried towards more orderly, more consistent, more integrated and more shared values.

This is the dynamic that is all the time acting so as to move us towards some cultural destination. Transaction theory's error, however, lies in its assumption that, because we are all being pulled towards a destination, there is only one destination, and this is where cultural theory comes in.

What we are being pulled towards, cultural theory tells us, is not a single destination but a *morphogenetic field* (Thom 1972): a quite complicated arrangement of attractors and repellers which ensures that there are always several different destinations - one for each of the forms of solidarity. So there are two dynamics at work: one that draws us towards the morphogenetic field and another that then carries us towards one or other of the attractors within that field. With these two dynamics in operation, and provided the first is acting faster than the second (otherwise we would drift away from the field faster than we were being carried across it[100]), then social life will proceed in such a way as always to generate the recurrent regularities which (apart from the hermit's) are so well captured by grid:group analysis (see, in particular, Gross and Rayner, 1985).

The essentials of this dynamical system are already summarised in Figure 3.2, where the five attractors correspond to the five solidarities, each of which will capture those who happen to find themselves on the right side of the separatrix that marks the line beyond which that attractor's attractiveness becomes less powerful than that of one of the other four. But *why* are the attractors and separatrices arranged in this way? The point (and it is a crucially important point) is this: if the attractors and separatrices *are* this way then all the problems raised by the grid:group scheme are resolved, but we will not have a proper theory until we have some plausible argument for this arrangement.

Since there is a lot at stake here - the very foundations of social science, I would say - I should first explain how it is that this arrangement of attractors and separatrices resolves all the problems that are raised by the grid:group scheme. Then, having done that, I will go on to the question of why the attractors and separatrices should be arranged in this particular way.

---

100 Which, of course, can happen: *anomie.*

- In the middle there is not a "grey mish-mash" but a fifth attractor: a fifth solidarity - the hermit's. And tiny shifts that are across a separatrix do result in a category change (because they bring the person under the thrall of a different attractor) whilst much larger shifts that happen not to cross a separatrix leave the solidarity unaltered.

- The hermit is now firmly on the "social map", in a central position: a zone within which each of the four patterns of relationships is sufficiently dismantled for it to be possible for it to then be built up into one of the other three.[101] Since there is no way of getting from any of these four to any one of the others without passing through this central zone, we can begin to see how it is that the hermit is not an "optional extra" in the cultural theory typology. If this central zone was not there then there would be no transitional niche (*the waiting room of history*, as Schmutzer had dubbed it) where the four "engaged" social beings can pause to change their spots, recharge their batteries, lick their wounds or do whatever it is that has to be done if they are to get from one corner to another. And, since cultural theory insists that there can be no stability without change, the hermit becomes a vital component of the whole dynamical system.

- The unit of analysis (as I have argued throughout) is the form of solidarity: the *pattern of social relationships*, together with the *shared set of beliefs and values* and the *behavioural strategy* that is rendered rational by those beliefs and values. This means that, if transactions fall into a number of fairly separate "spheres" (workplace and home, for instance, or the Swiss villager's communally owned pastures and private fields) then there is no reason why *an* individual cannot be a vital part of several different forms of solidarity. Of course, you cannot interview a form of solidarity - you have to talk to its constituent individuals - which is why (as Mary Douglas has always insisted) you have always to be sensitive to the *transactional context*. You do not want your individual to be

---

101 Topologists would point out that you cannot go gradually from a granny knot to a reef knot. But neither needs to be totally dismantled in order to get to the other; you only need to half undo it.

hopping about from one solidarity to another while you are trying to understand one of those solidarities by talking to him or her.

- Grid and group *are* orthogonal, in the sense that they have been very well chosen so as to capture the key conditions (*openness* and *strong connectedness*) which, Schmutzer and Bandler have shown, result in "truly distinct types that cannot be transformed into each other unless the principal conditions are altered".

Why are the Attractors and Separatrices Arranged in this Way?

Since this scheme of attractors and separatrices (see Figure 3.2) neatly extricates us from all the common objections that are raised by the grid:group diagram, it is certainly worth a second glance. And that second glance, of course, should light upon the possible reasons for these attractors and separatrices being the way the scheme has them.

There are two complementary ways of addressing ourselves to this question. We can ask what would be the simplest dynamical system that would generate the recurrent regularities that constitute the grid:group typology, and we can ask ourselves what it is that each of these solidarities is all the time doing to the others. We have already made some progress along both of these approaches in the preceding chapters. On the first, Schmutzer and Bandler's proof of the impossibility theorem has given us the five attractors and the key conditions in terms of which we can position them in relation to one another. On the second, the way in which each form of solidarity ceaselessly predates on the others, whilst ultimately depending on them for its very existence, has opened up some understanding of their interactions: their ability to self-organise and their non-extinguishability.

One of the oft-voiced objections to cultural theory is that it leaves out power. My response to this is that it couldn't! The sort of self-organisation that is inherent in the *requisite variety condition* - that each way of organising needs the others to organise itself against - simply would not happen if coercion was absent. Each way of organising, cultural theory insists, is viable only in an environment that contains the others, and it ensures its viability by inculcating in its constituent social beings the appropriate behavioural strategy. These strategies (as is explained in chapter 4, and at more length in Thompson, 1982) are *individualised manipulation* ("If I don't do it somebody else will", for instance) for the individualist, *collectivised manipulation* (differential maintenance by "working to rule", for instance) for the hierarchist, *collectivised survival* ("treading lightly on the Earth", for instance) for the egalitarian, and *individualised survival* ("If you know a better hole go to it", for instance) for the fatalist. The fact that two of these strategies are manipulative and two are survivalist suggests that each way of organising gets itself going by getting some sort of grip on the others: that there is a sort of action and reaction among them as the members of each behave rationally in the one world they all inhabit, each according to their convictions as to how that world is. Power, in other words, is an *emergent property* of this self-organising system.

Indeed a Canadian engineer, Nils Lind (personal communication), has taken Mary Douglas' analytical scheme and shown that this "third dimension" - he calls it *grip* - is an inevitable concomitant of her "two dimensions of sociality". Power, in other words, is part-and-parcel of organising and cannot therefore be left out by cultural theory.[102] Translating this insight into the language of dynamical systems, we can say that, associated with the *control space* that is depicted in Figure 3.2, there is a *behaviour space* which, as it were, captures the essential consequences of the interactions between the five ways of organising that are described by the control space.[103]

This particular behaviour space, fortunately (since we want to be able to depict it in diagram form), is uni-dimensional: the individualist and hierarchist strategies result in positive *grip*, the fatalist and egalitarian strategies in negative *grip*, and the hermit ends up at the one position that is not occupied by any of the others: zero *grip*. The result of all this is a morphogenetic field that has just five flat areas, each of which

---

102 Though, of course, some cultural theorists may not be *aware* of its entrainment.

103 It is the "behaviour" of the system, not the dividuals who constitute it, that is captured by this space, and it is the various shifts across Figure 3.2's two-dimensional space that "control" this behaviour. The terminology is of general validity and holds for all kinds of dynamical systems, not just those involving humans.

represents a viable strategy. Two are hilltops (the individualist's and the hierarchist's), two are valleys (the fatalist's and the egalitarian's) and one is a saddle-point (the hermit's)[104]:

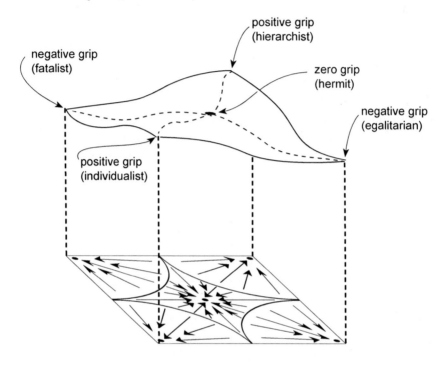

Figure 9.2: The morphogenetic field and its projection onto the control space.

So it is this three-dimensional "landscape" that depicts the morphogenetic field, and we can see that the diagram I have been using up till now (Figure 3.2) is simply the projection of this morphogenetic field down onto the control space. The import of all this, and the whole justification for my insisting that cultural theory be developed in the language and imagery of dynamical systems, is that it enables us to see why it is that the attractors and separatrices are arranged in this particular way. They *have* to be this way, given cultural theory's explicit requirements for each form of solidarity. In other words, cultural theory is saying

---

104 I should point out that if the two hilltops are on one diagonal and the two valleys on the other (which they are, given the Schmutzer and Bandler conditions) then there *has* to be a fifth attractor: the hermit's saddle-point.

much more than grid:group analysis, and it is only by setting it all out in dynamical systems terms that we can begin to understand what it is that it is saying.

This three dimensional surface, of course, depicts the *simplest* dynamical system. We could have "overhangs" (*cusp catastrophes*, as they are called) along any of the four sides of this morphogenetic field, which would result in sudden discontinuous transitions straight from one corner to an adjacent one without there always being a transitional hermit stage: Saul, for instance, going straight (and suddenly) from individualism to egalitarianism on the road to Damascus. And the surface itself could be changing its shape over time, in which case the behaviour space will be two-dimensional and this particular picture will be just one "still" from the whole. Such a two-dimensional behaviour space would allow for changes between positive and negative grip, as for instance happened when the egalitarian Khmer Rouge came to power in Cambodia. So this simplest system is almost certainly too simple. Indeed social systems, as JBS Haldane once remarked of natural systems, may be not just queerer than we imagine them to be but queerer than we *could* imagine them to be.

I will conclude by making some suggestions as to how we might begin to explore these more complicated (and imaginable) possibilities, but before I do that I should try to explain the mysterious force that carries us across the morphogenetic field to one or other of its five destinations: its five flat bits.

The Formation of Preferences

In carrying us to one or other of these five destinations this force results in our coming to know what it is that we want. This - the "emergence of cognition" - really *is* the central mystery of social science. Ask a roomful of economists how people get what they want and you will not be able to get another word in edgeways for hours (if not months or even years) but ask them where preferences come from and you will be able to hear a pin drop![105] Yet, for all the apparent unanswerability of this question,

---

105 The late Aaron Wildavsky actually did this, the roomful of economists being the committee that meets each year to decide who should receive the Nobel Prize for economics.

people (even the dimmest of people) *do* know what they want and what they do not want. Preference formation for humans, therefore, must be like migration for birds: they all do it, without thinking, but *how*?

As it happens, students of animal behaviour have recently made considerable progress in understanding these sorts of processes. The flocking behaviour of birds, for instance, which looks as though it could only come about through the continuous transmission of complicated and specific instructions to every single bird; can be realistically reproduced in computer simulation by programming all the "artificial" birds to follow just one very simple rule. That is how the pterodactyls did it in the film *Jurassic Park*,[106] and that, uncomplimentary though we may find it, is how we get our preferences!

Imagine a dim-witted crawling creature, equipped with only a spirit-level by way of sensory mechanism (no eyes, no ears, no touch, etc), and following just a single rule: "Always pull back from steepening slopes". Such a creature, plonked down at random onto the morphogenetic field (see Figure 9.2), would soon find its way to one of the five flat bits; which one, thanks to the separatrices, being determined by where it happened to be plonked down. And a whole lot of these creatures, scattered randomly across the landscape, would eventually end up clustered, some at one flat bit, others at another and so on.[107] So what *is* the spirit-level, and what *is* the single simple rule?

---

106 Strictly speaking, I should have said "flying animals", because pterodactyls are (or should I say were?) reptiles, not birds.

107 Since that would be the end of it (no more change) we need to think about what else must be going on if there is always to be some movement of dim-witted creatures between these flat bits. One plausible idea (which also enables us to have *grip* changing with time) is that the more crowded a flat bit becomes the less opportunity it affords to each of those who are clustered there. If you imagine the morphogenetic field to be made of some "smart" elasticated material that eventually reacts against the weight of the creatures it has to bear then a crowded flat bit will eventually implode, at which moment the strategies of those who are clustered there will no longer be stable.
Of course, those with poorer spirit-levels will become unstable sooner than the others, and their sudden departures will result in the "smart" material de-imploding. So not everyone is dislodged every time there is overcrowding. A computer simulation of this idea (as I have explained in chapter 6) gives us what cultural theory says we need: endless change without the permanent extinction of any of the destinations (Thompson and Tayler, 1985).

In earlier chapters I introduced the idea of attractors by listing a number of mutually contradictory proverbs and suggesting that if you gave heed to one of these proverbs you would come to know what you wanted, and get more of it, by moving in the direction that that proverb indicated. Of course, it will be objected that to discover our preferences in this way we have first to exercise a preference for one proverb rather than another, in which case we have not really explained the formation of preferences. But this idea of the dim-witted creature plonked down on the landscape gets around this objection. We do not *choose* the proverb; it is supplied to us by the landscape itself.

If proverbs are rules of thumb for the different solidarities ("Look before you leap" for hierarchy, for instance, and "He who hesitates is lost", for individualism) then what we have here is a way of understanding, first, what the spirit-level is and, second, what it is doing for us dim-witted creatures. As long as we always try to make transactional sense of where we happen to find ourselves, and as long as we have some way of telling the difference between more sense and less sense (that is, as long as we can tell steeper from shallower, and as long as we always plump for the shallower) then we will move ourselves to one of the five attractors. And, in the process of doing this, we will simultaneously establish our social relations and discover our preferences. And if we establish our relationships and pursue our preferences then we will have become social beings, and our various solidarities will have self-organised in the way cultural theory predicts. That, then, is all there is to it. Preference formation, like most mysteries once they have been revealed to you, is a bit of a let-down. Or is it?

Up There With The Pterodactyls

Discovering the simple "bottom-up" rule that enables our artificial pterodactyls to flock just like the real things[108] is no mean achievement, and cultural theory is now poised to do much the same for us. *Artificial social life* - playing around with dim-witted creatures and a few simple rules that even they are capable of following, and getting them to generate the rich, complicated and highly intelligent behaviours that we recognise as ours - promises a whole new dawn for social science: a new dawn in which the rising sun is the inherent relationality of the individual.

---

108 Or, rather, just like we imagine the real things flocked, nobody having actually seen them do it.

BIBLIOGRAPHY

Adams, J. (1995): *Risk*. London: UCL Press.

Angrist, S.W. (1991): Believers in one wave theory see US in deep trough soon. *The Wall Street Journal*, 8 August.

Ansoff, H. (1978): Planned Management of Turbulent Change. *European Institute for Advanced Studies in Management, Brussels. Working Paper 78-3.*

Arrow, K.J. (1951/63): *Social Choice and Individual Values.* New Haven and London: Yale University Press. (A much expanded second edition was published in 1963.)

Arthur, W.B. (1989): Competing technologies, increasing returns and lock-in by historical events: the dynamics of allocation under increasing returns. *Economic Journal, 99*: 116-131.

Astley, W. and Van der Ven, H. (1983): Central perspectives and debates in organisation theory. *Administrative Science Quarterly, 28*: 245-273.

Attenborough, D. (1984): Threat to the planet, *The Observer,* 1 April, London.

Barth, F. (1966): Models of social organisation. *Occasional Papers of the Royal Anthropological Institute, 23.*

Bentley, A. (1949): *The Process of Government.* Evanston, IL: Principa Press.

Bernstein, B. (1971): *Class, Codes and Control, vol 1.* London: Routledge and Kegan Paul.

Brion, D.J. (1992): The meaning of the city: urban redevelopment and the loss of community, *Indiana Law Review 25.3*: 685-740.

Burrell, G. and Morgan, G. (1979): *Sociological Paradigms and Organisational Analysis: Elements of the Sociology of Corporate Life.* London: Heinemann.

Chapman, G.P. and Thompson, M. (1995): *Water and the Quest for Sustainable Development in The Ganges Valley.* London: Mansell.

Clark, W.C. and Munn, R.E. (eds) (1986): *Sustainable Development of the Biosphere.* Cambridge: Cambridge University Press.

Clements, F.E. (1916): Plant succession: an analysis of the development of vegetation. *Carnegie Institute, Washington, Publication 242*: 1-512.

Cyert, R.M. and March, J.G. (1963): *A Behavioural Theory of the Firm.* Englewood Cliffs, NJ: Prentice-Hall.

Dake, K. and Thompson, M. (1993): The meanings of sustainable development: household strategies for managing needs and resources. *Human Ecology: Crossing Boundaries* (S.D. Wright, T. Dietz, R. Borden, G. Young and G. Guagnano, eds.) pp.421-436. Fort Collins, CO: The Society for Human Ecology.

Dake, K. and Thompson, M. (1999): Making ends meet: in the household and on the planet. *GeoJournal, 47*: 417-424.

Douglas, G. (1981): *Physics, Astrology and Semiotics.* London: Radical Astrology Group.

Douglas, M. (1970): *Natural Symbols.* London: Barrie and Rockcliff.

Douglas, M. (1982): (ed) *Essays in the Sociology of Perception.* London: Routledge and Kegan Paul.

Douglas, M. (2005): Grid and group revisited. *Paper presented in the complexity series: A Celebration of Cultural Theory, London School of Economics, 27 June.*

Douglas, M., Thompson, M. and Verweij, M. (2003): Is time running out? The case of global warming. *Daedalus, Spring*: 98-107.

Douglas, M. and Wildavsky, A. (1982): *Risk and Culture: An Essay on the Selection of Technical and Environmental Dangers.* Berkeley: University of California Press.

Durkheim, E. (1893): *De la Division du Travail Sociale: étude sur l'Organisation des Sociétés Supérieurs.* Paris: Alcan.

Eckholm, E.P. (1976): *Losing Ground: Environmental Stress and World Food Prospects.* New York: W.W. Norton and Co.

Ehrlich, P. and Holdren, J. (1974): Impact of population growth. *Science 171*: 1212-1217.

Elster, J. (1983): *Explaining Technical Change: A Case Study in the Philosophy of Science.* Cambridge: Cambridge University Press.

Elster, J. (1985): *Making Sense of Marx.* Cambridge: Cambridge University Press, and Paris: Editions de la Maison des Sciences de l'Homme.

Emery, F. and Trist, E. (1965): The causal texture of organisational environments. *Human Relations, 18.*

Evans-Wentz, W.Y. (1954): *The Tibetan Book of the Great Liberation.* London: Oxford University Press. pp.20-21.

Fischer, F. and Hajer, M.A. (1999): *Living With Nature: Environmental Politics as Cultural Discourse.* Oxford: Oxford University Press.

Forsyth,T. (2003): *Critical Political Ecology. The Politics of Environmental Science.* London: Routledge

Freeman, C. (ed) (1983): *Long Waves in the World Economy.* London: Butterworth.

Fripp, J. (1982): Problem-solving styles. *Journal of the Operational Research Society, 33(1).* pp.77-79.

Fürer-Haimendorf, C. von (1975): *Himalayan Traders: Life in Highland Nepal.* London: John Murray.

Gaskell, E. (1855): *North and South* (republished, in London, by Penguin in Penguin Classics, 1971).

Georgescu-Roegen, N. (1971): *The Entropy Law and The Economic Process.* Cambridge, MA: Harvard University Press.

Gleick, J (1987): *Chaos: Making a New Science.* London: Penguin, and New York: Viking-Penguin.

Grendstad, G. (1994): Classifying Cultures, PhD Thesis, University of Bergen, Norway.

Grendstad, G. and Selle, P. (1999): The formation and transformation of preferences: Cultural theory and postmaterialism compared. In Michael Thompson, Gunnar Grendstad and Per Selle (eds) *Cultural Theory as Political Science.* London: Routledge: 43-58.

Gross, J. and Rayner, S. (1985): *Measuring Culture: A Paradigm for the Analysis of Social Organisation.* New York: Columbia University Press.

Gyawali, D. (2000): Nepal-Indo Water resource relations, In I.W. Zartman and J.Z. Rubin (eds) *Power and Negotiation.* Ann Arbor: University of Michigan Press.

Gyawali, D. (2001): *Water in Nepal.* Lalitpur, Nepal: Himal Books. (International edition published by Zed Books, London, as *Rivers, Technology and Society.* 2003.)

Hardin, G. (1972): The tragedy of the commons. *Science, 162*: 1243-1248.

Hayek, F.A. (1944) *The Road to Serfdom.* London: Routledge and Kegan Paul.

Heiner, R. (1983): The origin of predictable behaviour. *American Economic Review, 73(4).* pp.560-595

Hendriks, F. (1994): Cars and culture in Munich and Birmingham: the case for cultural pluralism. In D.J. Coyle and R.J. Ellis (eds) *Politics, Policy and Culture.* Boulder, CO: West View Press.

Hendriks, F. (2006): *Vitale Democratie: Theorie van Democratie in Actie.* Amsterdam: Amsterdam University Press.

Hirt, P.W. (1994): *A Conspiracy of Optimism.* Lincoln, NE: Nebraska University Press.

Holling, C.S. (1986): the resilience of terrestrial ecosystems: local surprise and global change. *Sustainable Development of the Biosphere* (W.C. Clark and R.E. Munn, eds) pp.292-320. Cambridge: Cambridge University Press.

Holling, C.S., Gunderson, L. and Peterson, G. (1993): Comparing Ecological and Social Systems. *Beijer Discussion Paper Series No.36.* Beijer International Institute of Ecological Economics, Stockholm.

Hood, C. (1998): *The Art of the State: Culture, Rhetoric and Public Management.* Oxford: Clarendon Press.

Intriligator, M.D., Wedel, J.R. and Lee, C.H. (2006): What Russia can learn from China in its transition to a market economy. In M. Verweij and M. Thompson (eds) *Clumsy Solutions for a Complex World.* Basingstoke: Palgrave.

Jung, C. (1963): *Man and His Symbols* (ed. A. Jaffé). London: Picador.

Keynes, J.M. (1931): *Essays in Persuasion.* London: Macmillan.

Kolb, D. (1976): Management and the learning process. *California Management Review, 18(3).* pp.21-31.

Leach, M. and Mearns,R. (eds) (1996): *The Lie of the Land: Challenging Received Wisdom on the African Environment.* Oxford: James Currey

Lindblom, C. (1977): *Politics and Markets: The World's Political-Economic System.* New York: Basic Books.

Lockhart, C. (1997): Why environmental policy decisions are so controversial: rival cultural identities and disparate policy preferences. Paper, Department of Political Science, Texas Christian University.

Maine, H.S. (1861): *Ancient Law.* London: John Murray.

Mandelbrot, B. (1977): *The Fractal Geometry of Nature.* New York: Freeman.

March, J.G. and Olsen, J.P. (1989): *Rediscovering Institutions: The Organisational Basis of Politics.* New York and London: The Free Press.

March, J.G. and Olsen, J.P. (1995): *Democratic Governance.* New York: The Free Press.

Marriott, M. (1967): Hindu transactions: diversity without dualism. In B. Kapferer (ed) *Transaction and Meaning.* Philadelphia, Pennsylvania: Institute for the Study of Human Issues.

Marx, K. (1859): *Capital* (1967 edition published by Basic Books, New York).

May, R. (1972): Will a large complex system be stable? *Nature 238*: 413-414.

Mitroff, I., Kilmann, R. and Barabba, V. (1977): The application of behavioural and philosophical technologies to strategic planning: a case study with a large federal agency. *Management Science, 24(1)*. pp.44-58.

Namenwirth, Z. (1973): The wheels of time and the interdependence of value change. *Interdisciplinary History, 3*. pp.649-683.

Ney, S. (1997): Why is pension reform so difficult? The institutional limits to reforming social security. Paper presented at a joint LOS/ IIASA (Norwegian Research Centre in Organisation and Management/ International Institute for Applied Systems Analysis) meeting on "Security: Environmental and Social", Laxenburg, Austria, November.

Ney, S. (2006): Refurbishing Pluralism, doctoral thesis, University of Bergen, Norway.

Odum, E.P. (1969): The strategy of ecosystem development. *Science, 164*: 262-270.

Ostrander, D. (1982): One- and Two-dimensional models of the distribution of beliefs. In M. Douglas (ed) *Essays in the Sociology of Perception.* London: Routledge and Kegan Paul.

Ostrom, E. (1990): *Governing The Commons: The Evolution of Institutions for Collective Action.* New York: Cambridge University Press.

Overseas Development Agency (1997): *Natural Resource Research: Working for Development.* (Third report on the ODA's Renewable Natural Resources Research Strategy) ODA, London.

Parsons, T., Bales, R. and Shils, E. (1953): Phase movement in relation to motivation, symbol formation, and role structure. Ch.5 in *Working Papers in the Theory of Action*. New York: The Free Press.

Powell, W.W. and Dimaggio, P.J. (eds) (1991): *The New Institutionalism in Organisational Analysis*. Chicago and London: University of Chicago Press.

Price, M.F. and Thompson, M. (1996): The complex life: human land uses in mountain ecosystems. *Global Ecology and Biogeography Letters,* 6: 77-90.

Putnam, R.D. (1993): *Making Democracy Work: Civic Traditions in Modern Italy.* Princeton, NJ: Princeton University Press.

Rapoport, A. (1985): Uses of experimental games. In M. Grauer, M. Thompson and A. Wierzbicki (eds) *Plural Rationality and Interactive Decision Processes.* Berlin: Springer-Verlag.

Rayner, S. (2006): Wicked Problems, Clumsy Solutions. First Jack Beale Memorial Lecture, University of New South Wales, Sydney, Australia, 25 July.

Rayner, S. and Malone, E.L. (eds) (1998): *Human Choice and Climate Change (4 vols).* Columbus, Ohio: Battelle Press.

Rotmans, J. and de Vries, B. (1997): *Perpsectives on Global Change.* Cambridge: Cambridge University Press

Schmutzer, M.E.A. (1994): *Ingenium und Individuum. Eine sozialwissenschaftliche Theorie von Wissenschaft und Technik.* Wien, New York: Springer Verlag.

Schmutzer, M.E.A. and Bandler, K. (1980): Hi and low - in and out: approaches to social status. *Cybernetics, 10:* 283-299.

Schumacher, E.F. (1973): *Small is Beautiful: a Study of Economics as if People Mattered.* London: Blond and Briggs.

Schumpeter, J.A. (1911): *Theory of Capitalist Development.* (The English translation was published in 1934.)

Schumpeter, J.A. (1939): *Business Cycles.* (2vols). Philadelphia: Porcupine Press

Schumpeter, J.A. (1950): *Capitalism, Socialism and Democracy.* New York: Harper and Row.

Schwartz, B. (1991): A pluralistic model of culture. *Contemporary Sociology,* 20(5) pp.764-766.

Schwarz, M. and Thompson, M. (1990): *Divided We Stand: Redefining Politics, Technology and Social Choice*. Philadelphia, PA: University of Pennsylvania Press.

Simon, H. (1978): Rationality as process and as product of thought. *American Economic Review Papers and Proceedings, 68*: 1-16.

Skidelsky, R. (2000): *John Maynard Keynes: Fighting for Britain 1937-1946*. London: Macmillan.

Smith, J.M. (1982): *Evolution and the Theory of Games*. Cambridge: Cambridge University Press.

Sugden, R. (1986): *The Economics of Rights, Co-operation and Welfare*. Oxford: Basil Blackwell.

Szreter, S. and Woolcock, M. (2004): Health by association? Social capital, social theory and the political economy of public health. *International Journal of Epidemiology, 33*: 650-667.

Tayler, P. (c.1986): Fourfold Patterns: Connecting Scale and Complexity in the Evolutionary Cycle. Working Paper No.5 of the Institute for Management Research and Development, University of Warwick, Coventry CV4 7AL, UK.

Thom, R. (1975): *Structural Stability and Morphogenesis* (French edition 1972) trans. D.H. Fowler. New York: Benjamin.

Thompson, M. (1976): Out with the boys again. Mountain 50. Reprinted in K. Wilson (ed) (1978) *The Games Climbers Play*. London: Diadem Books pp.344-353.

Thompson, M. (1982): "A three-dimensional model" and "The problem of the centre: an autonomous cosmology", both in Mary Douglas (ed) *Essays in the Sociology of Perception*. London: Routledge and Kegan Paul. pp.31-63 and 302-328.

Thompson, M. (1992): The dynamics of Cultural Theory and their implications for the enterprise culture, in Sean Hargreaves Heap and Angus Ross (eds) *Understanding the Enterprise Culture*. pp.182-202. Edinburgh: Edinburgh University Press.

Thompson, M. (1997): Cultural theory and integrated assessment. *Environmental Modelling and Assessment 2*: 139-150.

Thompson, M. (2002): Man and nature as a single but complex system. In Ted Munn (ed-in-chief) *Encyclopedia of Global Environmental Change, vol.5*, Chichester: John Wiley 384-393.

Thompson, M., Ellis, R. and Wildavsky, A. (1990): *Cultural Theory.* Boulder, CO and Oxford: West View.

Thompson, M. and Gyawali, D. (2007): Uncertainty revisited or the triumph of hype over experience. New introduction to the republished M. Thompson, M. Warburton and T. Hatley, *Uncertainty on a Himalayan Scale.* Lalitpur, Nepal: Himal Books.

Thompson, M., Rayner, S. and Ney, S. (1998): Risk and governance part 2: policy in a complex and plurally perceived world. *Government and Opposition 33.3*: 139-166.

Thompson, M. and Tayler, P. (1985): The Surprise Game: An Exploration of Constrained Relativism. Working Paper of the Institute for Management Research and Development, University of Warwick, Coventry CV4 7AL, UK.

Thompson, M., Verweij, M. and Ellis, R.J. (2006): Why and how culture matters. In R.E. Goodin and C. Tilly (eds) *The Oxford Handbook of Contextual Political Analysis.* Oxford: Oxford University Press.

Thompson, M., Warburton, M. and Hatley, T. (1986): *Uncertainty on a Himalayan Scale.* London: Ethnographica.

Thompson, M. and Wildavsky, A. (1986): A cultural theory of information bias in organisations. *Management Studies 23(3).* pp.273-286.

Tilly, C. (2006): How and why trust networks work. In C. Tilly (ed) *Trust and Rule.* Cambridge: Cambridge University Press.

Tomkins, S. (1989): *Forestry in Crisis.* London: Christopher Helm.

Tönnies, F. (1887): Gemeinschaft und Gesellschaft, Darmstadt: Wissenschaftlich (translated by C.P. Loomis, 1957, as *Community and Society.* East Lansing, MI: Michigan State University Press

Turner B.L. Clark, W.C., Kates, R.W., Richards, J.F., Matthews, J.T., Meyer, W.B. et al (1990): *The Earth as Transformed by Human Action.* New York: Cambridge University Press.

Ulanowicz, R. (1979): Complexity, stability and self-organisation in natural communities. *Oecologia 43(3).* pp.295-298.

Ulanowicz, R. (1980): An hypothesis on the development of natural communities. *Theoretical Biology 85*. pp.223-245.

Utterback, J. and Abernethy, W. (1975): A dynamic model of process and product innovation. *Omega 3(6)*. pp.639-656.

Verweij, M. (2000): *Transboundary Environmental Problems and Cultural Theory: The Protection of the Rhine and the Great Lakes*. Basingstoke and New York: Palgrave Macmillan

Verweij, M. (2001): Forget the Hague: curb global warming instead. Seminar paper presented at IIASA (International Institute for Applied Systems Analysis) Laxenburg, Austria, 18 January. (A similar argument is set out in M. Verweij: Is the Kyoto Protocol merely irrelevant, or positively harmful, for the efforts to curb climate change? in Verweij and Thompson, 2006, op cit.)

Verweij, M. (2007): Unpublished teaching aid "Grid and Group Galore", Department of International Relations Jacobs University, Bremen, Germany. See Hendriks (2006) for a number of the mappings this teaching aid draws on.

Verweij, M. and Thompson, M. (eds) (2006): *Clumsy Solutions for a Complex World*. Basingstoke: Palgrave.

Weber, M. (1992): Wirtschaft und Gesselschaft, Tübingen: Mohr. Translated by E. Bischoff et al (1978) *Economy and Society: An Outline of Interpretive Sociology*. Berkeley: University of California Press.

Weber, R. (1981): Society and economy in the Western world system. *Social Forces 59*. pp.1130-1148.

Williamson, O. (1975): *Markets and Hierarchies, Analysis and Anti-Trust Implications: A Study in the Economics of Internal Organisation*. New York: The Free Press.

Wynne, B. and Otway, H.J. (1982): Information technology, power and managers. In N. Bjorn-Anderson et al (eds) *Information Society: For Richer For Poorer*. Amsterdam: North-Holland.

Young, A. (1976): *The Geometry of Meaning*. Delacorte Press.

Zeeman, E.C. (1977): *Catastrophe Theory: Selected Papers 1972-1977*. Reading, MA and London: Addison-Wesley Publishing Company.

About the Author

Originally a professional soldier, Michael Thompson studied anthropology (University College London and Oxford) while also following a career as a Himalayan mountaineer (Annapurna South Face 1970, Everest Southwest Face 1975). His early research on how something second-hand becomes an antique, or a rat-infested slum part of Our Glorious Heritage ("Rubbish Theory", Oxford University Press 1979) diverted him into teaching at the Slade School of Fine Art, London and at Portsmouth University's School of Architecture, and from there to the International Institute for Applied Systems Analysis (IIASA), an East-West think-tank in Austria. There he worked on energy futures, on risk perception and on environment and development in the Himalayan Region, the key unifying concept in all that being "plural rationality": people doing very different things and yet still behaving rationally, given their different sets of convictions as to how the world is and people are ("Cultural Theory", with Richard Ellis and Aaron Wildavsky, West View, 1990; "Divided We Stand", with Michiel Schwarz, University of Pennsylvania Press, 1990).

Plural rationality, it transpired, tied in with two other "made at IIASA" concepts: "resilience" (developed by Buzz Holling, a Canadian ecologist) and "technological lock-in" (developed by Brian Arthur, an Irish economist) although it took Thompson a couple of decades, and lengthy stints in Unilever's Port Sunlight Research Laboratory, at Bergen University's Norwegian Centre for Management and Organisation, and at Oxford University's James Martin Institute for Science and Civilization to get from these connections to the notion of "clumsiness": all the voices (all the rationalities, that is) heard, and responded to by the others, in the policy process ("Clumsy Solutions for a Complex World", edited with Marco Verweij, Palgrave, 2006).

Michael Thompson is now back at IIASA, teasing out the various ideas of fairness that underpin the different rationalities and that are so seldom given adequate recognition in global-level decision-making, devising ways of clumsifying (and democratizing) international development aid, and enquiring into how urban infrastructures (those, for instance, that handle human waste by putting it into the water cycle) can be re-engineered so as to make cities into "forces for environmental good".

About Triarchy Press

Triarchy Press is an independent publishing house that looks at how organisations work and how to make them work better. We present challenging perspectives on organisations in short and pithy, but rigorously argued, books.

We have published a number of books by authors who come from a Systems Thinking background. These include: *The Three Ways Of Getting Things Done* by Gerard Fairtlough; *Management F-Laws* by Russell Ackoff, Herb Addison and Sally Bibb; *Systems Thinking in the Public Sector* by John Seddon and *Erasing Excellence* (published in the USA as *Liberating the Schoolhouse*) by Wellford Wilms.

Through our books, viewpoints, e-publications and discussion area, we aim to stimulate ideas by encouraging real debate about organisations in partnership with people who work in them, research them or just like to think about them.

Please tell us what you think about the ideas in this book. Join the discussion at:

www.triarchypress.com/telluswhatyouthink

If you feel inspired to write - or have already written - an article, a viewpoint or a book on any aspect of organisational theory or practice, we'd like to hear from you. Submit a proposal at:

www.triarchypress.com/writeforus

For more information about Triarchy Press and Systems Thinking, or to order any of our publications, please visit our website or drop us a line:

www.triarchypress.com
info@triarchypress.com

Printed in the United Kingdom
by Lightning Source UK Ltd.
135014UK00001B/130-204/P